Especially for

....

From

....

Date

....

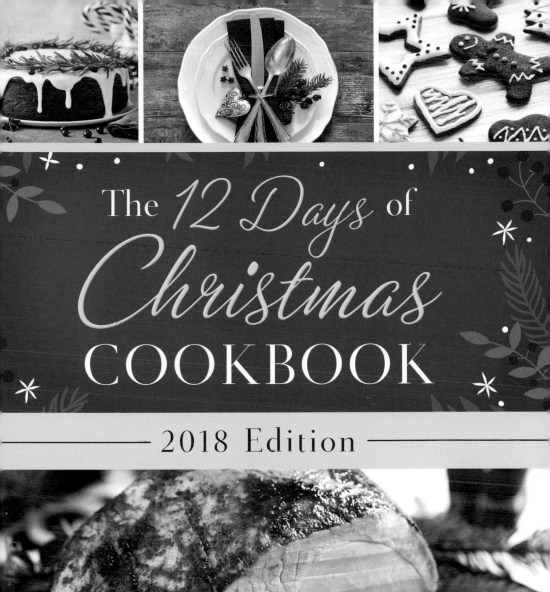

The *12 Days* of *Christmas* COOKBOOK

2018 Edition

BARBOUR BOOKS
An Imprint of Barbour Publishing, Inc.

Published by Barbour Books, an imprint of Barbour Publishing, Inc., 1810 Barbour Drive, Uhrichsville, Ohio 44683, www.barbourbooks.com

Our mission is to inspire the world with the life-changing message of the Bible.

ⒺⒸⓅⒶ Member of the
Evangelical Christian
Publishers Association

Printed in China.

Contents

Introduction

On the first day of Christmas my true love sent to me...

The holidays are about so many things—celebrating the birth of our Savior, affirming family bonds and treasured friendships, as well as passing along family values and traditions. What does that have to do with food? *Everything!* During the holidays, family recipes take on an almost magical quality, bringing us together and reminding us of our many blessings.

This year, along with many new recipes, we are celebrating some of the best recipes from our past *12 Days of Christmas* cookbooks. These "best" recipes will be noted with an icon (✳). We hope some of these have already become mainstays in your homes for Christmas.

*Heavenly Father, thank You for the gift of family and
all the ways You have given us to show our love for them.
Thank You also for the gift of Your Son, Jesus, without
whom we would not know love at all! Amen.*

On the first day of Christmas my true love sent to me:

An Appetizer on a Platter

The smells of Christmas are
the smells of childhood.

RICHARD PAUL EVANS

Father God, You grace us with Your love and kindness
all year long, but we feel it most dearly at Christmas when
we celebrate Your great sacrifice—the gift of Your Son, Jesus.
Thank You for the greatest gift ever given! Amen.

When the kindness and love of God our Savior appeared,
he saved us, not because of righteous things
we had done, but because of his mercy.

Titus 3:4–5 niv

Party Pecans *

1 egg white

1 teaspoon water

1 pound pecan halves

1 cup sugar

1 teaspoon cinnamon

1 teaspoon salt

Preheat oven to 225 degrees. In large bowl, whip egg white and water to froth. Add pecans and coat well. In separate bowl, combine sugar, cinnamon, and salt. Add to pecans, mixing with fingers to make sure pecans are well coated. Shake off excess sugar mixture and spread on foil-lined cookie sheet. Bake for 60 to 90 minutes, stirring every 15 minutes. Cool on baking sheet. Pecans will crisp up as they cool.

YIELD: 2 CUPS

Reindeer Bites *

❧ ⟶⟫⟨⟩⟫⟨⟩ ⟫⟨⟩⟫⟨⟩⟫⟨⟩ ⟫⟨⟩⟫⟨⟩ ❧

12 pitted dates	4 strips bacon
12 cashews	

Stuff dates with cashews. Cut each strip of bacon crosswise into 3 short portions. Wrap one around each date and secure with toothpick. Fry until done over medium-high heat.

YIELD: 12 SERVINGS

Party Nibbles *

2 cups toasted oats cereal

2 cups wheat squares cereal

2 cups pretzel sticks

1 cup shoestring potatoes

1 pound salted mixed nuts

1 pound butter, melted

1 teaspoon garlic salt

½ teaspoon onion salt

1 teaspoon seasoned salt

3 tablespoons Worcestershire sauce

Preheat oven to 250 degrees. In large bowl, toss together first 5 ingredients. Stir melted butter and seasonings together and pour over dry mixture, stirring well to coat. Spread onto parchment-lined cookie sheets and bake for 2 hours, stirring every half hour.

YIELD: 8 QUARTS

Nutty Honey Brie *

1 (8 ounce) round Brie cheese

¼ cup butter

¼ cup packed brown sugar

¼ cup chopped pecans

1 tablespoon honey

Preheat oven to 350 degrees. Place Brie in shallow pie plate and bake for 10 minutes. In saucepan, combine butter, brown sugar, pecans, and honey. Bring to boil over medium heat, stirring constantly. Pour sauce over Brie. Cut into wedges.

YIELD: 4 TO 8 SERVINGS

Minced Clam and Cheese Dip

1 clove garlic

1 (10 ounce) can minced clams

2 (4 ounce) packages cream cheese,
softened

¼ teaspoon salt

¼ teaspoon pepper

1 bag thick potato chips

Rub small bowl with garlic clove. Drain clams and reserve juice. In bowl, mix cream cheese with small amount of clam juice until smooth. Add clams, salt, and pepper. Stir well. Serve with potato chips.

YIELD: 1 CUP

Holiday Cheese Puffs

3 egg whites

1 cup shredded cheddar cheese

1 tablespoon flour

½ teaspoon salt

¼ teaspoon garlic powder

1 cup saltine cracker crumbs

Preheat oven to 350 degrees. In large bowl, beat egg whites until stiff. In separate bowl, combine cheese, flour, salt, and garlic powder. Fold cheese mixture into egg whites. Form into walnut-size balls. Roll each ball in cracker crumbs. Bake for 25 minutes or until golden brown.

YIELD: 6 SERVINGS

Fancy Ham and Cheese Ball

2 (8 ounce) packages cream cheese, softened

4 ounces crumbled blue cheese

¼ teaspoon red pepper flakes

1 (5 ounce) can chunk ham, drained

¼ cup minced chives

1 cup finely chopped pecans, toasted

Chips or crackers

In medium bowl, beat together cream cheese, blue cheese, and red pepper flakes at medium speed until smooth. Stir in ham and chives. Shape into ball and roll in pecans. Cover and chill overnight. Serve with chips or crackers.

YIELD: 1 (4 INCH) CHEESE BALL

Merry Marinated Mushrooms

1 pound cremini mushrooms

¼ cup lemon juice

½ cup olive oil

¼ cup chopped parsley

¾ teaspoon salt

1¼ teaspoons ground pepper

2 green onions, thinly sliced

1 clove garlic, finely chopped

¼ teaspoon paprika

Cut mushrooms into ⅛-inch slices. In large bowl, mix mushrooms with lemon juice. Stir in oil, parsley, salt, pepper, onions, and garlic. Toss. Cover and refrigerate for 3 hours, stirring occasionally. Just before serving, remove mushrooms with slotted spoon and sprinkle with paprika.

YIELD: 10 SERVINGS

Pizza Bites

2 tablespoons butter, softened

½ teaspoon minced garlic

3 English muffins, split and toasted

24 slices pepperoni

12 cherry tomatoes, cut in half

1 cup shredded mozzarella cheese

½ teaspoon dried oregano

Mix butter and garlic. Spread on muffin halves. Slice each muffin into 4 wedges without cutting whole way through. Place 1 slice pepperoni and 1 tomato on each wedge. Place in broiler pan. Mix cheese and oregano. Sprinkle over muffin wedges. Broil until cheese is melted, about 2 minutes. Cut through wedges before serving.

YIELD: 6 SERVINGS

Pecan Cheese Ball

1 (8 ounce) package cream cheese, room temperature

3 tablespoons sweet onion relish

2 tablespoons steak sauce

1 teaspoon pepper sauce

⅛ teaspoon garlic powder

1½ cups chopped pecans, divided

Mix cheese together with onion relish, steak sauce, pepper sauce, garlic powder, and 1 cup pecans. Form into ball and chill. Before serving, roll in remaining pecans. Serve with chips or crackers.

YIELD: 1 (4 INCH) BALL

Santa's Shrimp Dip

1 (8 ounce) package cream cheese, softened

1 (6 ounce) carton plain yogurt

1 tablespoon diced chives

1 teaspoon prepared horseradish

¼ teaspoon salt

1 (4.5 ounce) can small shrimp, drained and rinsed

Crackers or toasted bread pieces

In medium bowl, mix together cream cheese, yogurt, chives, horseradish, and salt. Cream thoroughly. Add shrimp. Stir to mix well. Cover and refrigerate for 2 hours. Serve with crackers or toasted bread pieces.

YIELD: 2 CUPS

Crazy Spread

1 cup pecans

2 hard-boiled eggs

1 medium onion

1 (4.5 ounce) jar olives

1 cup mayonnaise

½ teaspoon garlic salt

¼ teaspoon cayenne pepper

Crackers or toast points

Combine pecans, eggs, onion, and olives in food processor. Add mayonnaise, garlic salt, and cayenne pepper. Cream well. Spread on crackers or toast points.

YIELD: 3 CUPS

Creamy Christmas Avocado Dip

2 ripe avocados, peeled and diced

1 medium onion, finely chopped (½ cup)

1 green chili pepper, finely chopped

1 tablespoon lemon juice

1 teaspoon salt

½ teaspoon coarsely ground pepper

1 medium tomato, finely chopped (about ¾ cup)

1 medium bag corn chips

Beat avocados, onion, chili pepper, lemon juice, salt, and pepper until creamy. Stir in tomato. Cover and refrigerate for at least 1 hour. Serve with corn chips.

YIELD: 2 CUPS

Saucy Meatballs in Cranberry Sauce

1 pound seasoned pork sausage

2 eggs, beaten

1 cup bread crumbs

1 teaspoon salt

½ teaspoon poultry seasoning

1 (16 ounce) can cranberry sauce

1 tablespoon mustard

Preheat oven to 350 degrees. In medium bowl, combine sausage, eggs, bread crumbs, salt, and poultry seasoning. Shape into 1-inch balls. Bake for 30 minutes. Combine cranberry sauce and mustard in medium saucepan. Heat until melted. Add sausage balls. Cover and simmer 15 minutes.

YIELD: 30 MEATBALLS

Nutty Holiday Meatballs

½ cup peanut butter

½ pound ground beef

¼ cup finely chopped onion

2 tablespoons chili sauce

1 teaspoon salt

1 teaspoon sage

⅛ teaspoon pepper

½ cup quick-cooking oats

1 egg, beaten

⅓ cup evaporated milk

2 (8 ounce) cans tomato sauce

1 teaspoon garlic salt

½ teaspoon oregano

¼ teaspoon pepper

¼ cup water

Preheat oven to 350 degrees. In large bowl, combine peanut butter, beef, onion, chili sauce, salt, sage, pepper, oats, egg, and milk. Shape beef mixture into balls (about 30). Place on foil-covered cookie sheet and bake for 25 minutes. Pour off drippings. In large saucepan, combine tomato sauce, garlic salt, oregano, pepper, and water. Add meatballs. Cover and simmer for 15 minutes. Serve with wooden picks.

YIELD: 30 MEATBALLS

Baked Chestnuts

1 pound bacon, strips cut into thirds

1 can water chestnuts

¼ cup brown sugar

Preheat oven to 350 degrees. Wrap piece of bacon around each water chestnut. Stick toothpick in each and place on foil-covered jelly roll pan. Sprinkle each lightly with brown sugar. Bake for 20 minutes.

YIELD: 30 CHESTNUTS

Sausage Cranberry Dip

1 (6 ounce) can whole cranberry sauce

2 tablespoons honey

1 tablespoon Worcestershire sauce

1 tablespoon lemon juice

1 clove garlic, minced

2 pounds smoked Polish sausage

Assorted party crackers

In medium saucepan, combine cranberry sauce, honey, Worcestershire, lemon juice, and garlic. Bring mixture to boil. Reduce heat and simmer, covered, for 5 minutes. Slice sausage and cut into small bits. In medium skillet, cook until brown. Add to cranberry sauce mixture and serve with assorted party crackers.

YIELD: 2 CUPS

Reindeer Reuben Snacks

1 cup finely chopped cooked
   corned beef

1 cup drained sauerkraut

1 cup shredded swiss cheese

½ teaspoon caraway seed

1 (7.5 ounce) tube refrigerator biscuits

¼ cup milk

1 (8 ounce) envelope chicken
   coating mix

Preheat oven to 400 degrees. In small bowl, combine corned beef, sauerkraut, cheese, and caraway seed. Roll out each biscuit into 4-inch circle. Place 2 tablespoons beef mixture on center of each. Fold over to enclose filling. Seal edges. Dip each in milk and then coating mix. Place on ungreased baking sheet. Bake for 10 minutes. Turn over and bake for another 10 minutes.

YIELD: 10 SERVINGS

Festive Oriental Nuts

2 (3.25 ounce) packages blanched
whole almonds

1 (7 ounce) can dry roasted cashews

1 teaspoon soy sauce

1 teaspoon water

2 tablespoons butter

1 teaspoon five-spice powder

⅛ teaspoon garlic powder

Preheat oven to 350 degrees. Place nuts in 15x10-inch jelly roll pan. Mix soy sauce and water. Drizzle sauce over nuts, tossing to distribute evenly. Dot with butter. Bake for 10 minutes. Mix spice powder and garlic powder together. Sprinkle over nuts. Bake uncovered, stirring occasionally, for 8 to 10 additional minutes.

Yield: 10 servings

Seven-Layer Christmas Dip

1 (15 ounce) can refried beans

1 (12 ounce) tub guacamole dip

1 (1.25 ounce) package taco seasoning mix

1 (8 ounce) package cream cheese, softened

1 pound ground beef, browned and drained

1 medium tomato, chopped

1 cup shredded cheddar cheese

1 (2.25 ounce) can sliced black or green olives

Corn chips

In large bowl, layer ingredients as follows: refried beans then guacamole dip. In small bowl, mix together taco seasoning and cream cheese. Add cream cheese layer over guacamole. Add layer of ground beef followed by layer of tomato. Sprinkle with cheese and top with olives. Chill in refrigerator for 2 hours. Serve with corn chips.

Yield: 25 servings

Recipe: ....

Ingredients: ....

....

....

....

Directions: ....

....

....

....

....

....

Yield: ....

Recipe: ....

Ingredients: ....

....

....

....

Directions: ....

....

....

....

....

Yield: ....

Recipe: ....

INGREDIENTS: ....

....

....

DIRECTIONS: ....

....

....

....

....

YIELD: ....

Recipe: ....

INGREDIENTS: ....

....

....

DIRECTIONS: ....

....

....

....

....

YIELD: ....

Recipe: ....

INGREDIENTS: ....

....

....

DIRECTIONS: ....

....

....

....

....

YIELD: ....

Two Beverages a-Blending

Christmas is the gentlest, loveliest festival
of the revolving year—and yet, for all that,
when it speaks, its voice has strong authority.

W. J. CAMERON

Lord God, our hearts are filled with praise for You. We pray that our praise is a worthy gift, for it comes from our surrendered hearts. Thank You for opening Your heart to us when we had no gift to offer. Amen.

By grace you have been saved through faith; and that not of yourselves, it is the gift of God.

Ephesians 2:8 nasb

Pineapple Orange Fizzes *

1 (8 ounce) glass crushed ice

3 cups orange juice

1 (8 ounce) can crushed pineapple, undrained

1 liter ginger ale

In blender, combine ice, orange juice, and pineapple. Blend until smooth. Fill serving glasses half full. Add cold ginger ale to fill glass. Stir gently and serve.

YIELD: 6 CUPS

Minty Christmas Creams *

2 cups crushed ice

2 ounces crème de menthe

4 ounces crème de cacao

6 generous scoops vanilla ice cream

In blender, combine ice, crème de menthe, crème de cacao, and ice cream. Blend until well mixed and smooth.

YIELD: 4 CUPS

Christmas Eve Cocktail *

2 cups unsweetened pineapple juice

1 cup tomato juice

Juice of 2 lemons

4 mint sprigs

In 1-quart pitcher, combine pineapple juice, tomato juice, and lemon juice. Let stand for 1 hour. Chill for additional hour. Pour into cocktail glasses and garnish with sprig of mint.

YIELD: 4 SERVINGS

Granny Nell's Hot Spiced Cider *

8 cups apple cider

¼ cup packed brown sugar

6 cinnamon sticks

1 teaspoon whole allspice

1 teaspoon whole cloves

1 (6 inch) piece cheesecloth

Kitchen string

1 orange, thinly sliced

In saucepan, combine cider and brown sugar. Prepare spice bag by placing cinnamon sticks, allspice, and cloves onto cheesecloth. Bring corners together and tie with string. Add bag to cider mixture. Bring to boil. Reduce heat, cover, and simmer for 10 minutes. Remove and discard spice bag. Pour into mugs and garnish with orange slices.

YIELD: 8 SERVINGS

Mint Sparkle

1 (20 ounce) jar mint jelly

2 cups water, divided

2 (12 ounce) cans unsweetened
pineapple juice

½ cup lemon juice

1 (12 ounce) bottle ginger ale, chilled

In medium saucepan, combine jelly and 1 cup water. Cook over low heat, stirring constantly, until jelly melts. Let cool. Stir in pineapple juice, remaining 1 cup water, and lemon juice. Chill thoroughly. Just before serving, pour into punch bowl and gently stir in ginger ale.

YIELD: 2 QUARTS

Christmas Dream Punch

½ cup heavy cream

2 cups frozen strawberries, partially
thawed

1 cup crushed pineapple

1 cup ginger ale

In blender, combine cream, strawberries, and pineapple. Process at high speed until smooth. Add ginger ale. Pour into chilled glasses. Serve immediately.

YIELD: 6 SERVINGS

Banana Slush Punch

4 cups sugar

6 cups boiling water

Juice of 2 lemons

1 (46 ounce) can pineapple juice

1 (6 ounce) can frozen orange juice concentrate

5 bananas, pureed

3 quarts ginger ale

In large pot, dissolve sugar in boiling water. Add lemon juice, pineapple juice, orange juice concentrate, and bananas, mixing well. Freeze until firm. Place in punch bowl. Let stand at room temperature for 30 minutes. Stir in ginger ale until slushy. Serve immediately.

YIELD: 50 SERVINGS

Sparkling Holiday Punch

1 quart cranberry juice cocktail

1 (6 ounce) can frozen orange juice
  concentrate, thawed (undiluted)

1 (6 ounce) can frozen lemonade
  concentrate, thawed (undiluted)

2 cups water

Ice

2 cups ginger ale

In large pitcher, combine cranberry juice cocktail, orange juice concentrate, lemonade concentrate, and water. Chill. Just before serving, pour juice mixture over ice in punch bowl. Slowly stir in ginger ale.

YIELD: 2½ QUARTS

Holiday Hot Chocolate

½ cup sugar

¼ cup cocoa

⅓ cup water

½ teaspoon cinnamon

¼ teaspoon nutmeg

4 cups milk

¾ cup marshmallow crème

In 2-quart saucepan, heat sugar, cocoa, water, cinnamon, and nutmeg over low heat, stirring constantly, until mixture is smooth. Bring to boil, reduce heat, and simmer for 4 minutes, stirring constantly. Stir in milk. Heat mixture over low heat. Pour into mugs and top each with 2 tablespoons marshmallow crème.

YIELD: 6 SERVINGS

Winter Watermelon Smash

3 cups watermelon, pitted and diced

¼ cup light corn syrup

2 tablespoons lime juice

2 teaspoons nonfat dry milk

1 cup sparkling white grape juice

6 ice cubes

In blender, combine watermelon, corn syrup, lime juice, dry milk, white grape juice, and ice cubes. Blend on high for 1 minute.

YIELD: 5 SERVINGS

New Year's Floats

3 cups grape juice

½ cup lemon juice

1 cup apple cider

¼ cup sugar

1 cup ginger ale

1 pint orange sherbet

In large pitcher, combine grape juice, lemon juice, cider, and sugar. Just before serving, add ginger ale. Fill glasses about ¾ full and top each with scoop of orange sherbet. Serve immediately.

YIELD: 6 SERVINGS

Hot Spiced Milk

¼ cup sweetened flaked coconut

1 tablespoon butter, melted

4 cups milk

½ teaspoon cinnamon

½ teaspoon nutmeg

2 tablespoons honey

In 3-quart saucepan, cook coconut in melted butter, stirring to brown evenly. Add milk, cinnamon, nutmeg, and honey. Heat to scalding. Strain out coconut and serve immediately.

YIELD: 5 SERVINGS

Tomato Juice Cocktail

1 quart tomato juice

¾ teaspoon Worcestershire sauce

½ teaspoon salt

½ teaspoon sugar

1 teaspoon lemon juice

1 teaspoon cider vinegar

½ teaspoon prepared horseradish

¼ teaspoon celery salt

In large pitcher, combine tomato juice, Worcestershire, salt, sugar, lemon juice, vinegar, horseradish, and celery salt. Mix thoroughly. Chill until ready to serve.

YIELD: 1 QUART

Caramel Eggnog

8 tablespoons sugar, divided

1½ cups boiling water

3 eggs, separated

3 cups milk

¾ cup evaporated milk, chilled

¼ teaspoon salt

In medium skillet, heat 6 tablespoons sugar, stirring frequently until it becomes amber liquid. Slowly add boiling water and stir until caramel dissolves. Remove from heat and chill. Just before serving, beat egg yolks until very thick and lemon yellow. Beat egg whites separately, gradually adding 2 tablespoons sugar, until very stiff and smooth. In large bowl, combine chilled caramel syrup with milk and evaporated milk. Fold egg whites into yolks, and quickly stir in salt and milk mixture. Serve immediately.

Yield: 5 servings

Saucy Spiced Cider

1 quart apple cider

¼ cup packed brown sugar

½ teaspoon whole cloves

½ teaspoon whole allspice

1 cinnamon stick

¼ teaspoon salt

In 2-quart saucepan, combine cider, brown sugar, cloves, allspice, cinnamon stick, and salt over medium heat. Stir constantly, but do not boil. Let mixture set for 5 minutes. Strain cider to remove spices. Serve hot.

YIELD: 4 SERVINGS

Cranberry Float

1 quart cranberry juice, chilled

½ cup orange juice, chilled

1 tablespoon lemon juice

2 cups ginger ale, chilled

1 pint orange sherbet

In medium punch bowl, combine cranberry juice, orange juice, and lemon juice. Pour in ginger ale. Top with small scoops of sherbet.

YIELD: 14 SERVINGS

Pink Party Punch

3 tablespoons red cinnamon candies

¼ cup sugar

½ cup warm water

1 (46 ounce) can pineapple juice, chilled

1 (32 ounce) can ginger ale, chilled

In small saucepan, combine cinnamon candies, sugar, and water. Bring to boil, reduce heat, and simmer, stirring occasionally, until candy dissolves. In large punch bowl, combine candy mixture with pineapple juice. Stir well. Gently stir in ginger ale just before serving.

YIELD: 2½ QUARTS

Christmas Morning Tea

2 cups boiling water

5 regular tea bags

¼ teaspoon ground cinnamon

¼ teaspoon ground nutmeg

⅓ cup sugar

1 (48 ounce) bottle cranberry
  juice cocktail

½ cup orange juice

½ cup water

¼ cup lemon juice

In large glass measuring cup, pour boiling water over tea bags. Add cinnamon and nutmeg. Let steep for 5 minutes. Remove tea bags, squeezing each gently. Add sugar. Stir until sugar dissolves. Pour into 3-quart pitcher. Add cranberry juice, orange juice, water, and lemon juice. Serve while warm.

YIELD: 2 QUARTS

Café Espresso

2 cups sugar

4 cups boiling water

4 teaspoons instant espresso coffee
   granules

2 cups hot water

½ cup crème de cacao

1 pint vanilla ice cream

In large saucepan, dissolve sugar in boiling water. In large glass measuring cup, dissolve coffee granules in hot water. In separate container, combine sugar and coffee mixtures. Blend well. Freeze for 8 hours or until slushy. Stir in crème de cacao. Spoon into 6 cups and top each with scoop of ice cream.

Yield: 6 servings

My Favorite Christmas Beverage Recipes

Recipe: ....

INGREDIENTS: ....

DIRECTIONS: ....

YIELD: ....

Recipe: ....

INGREDIENTS: ....

DIRECTIONS: ....

YIELD: ....

Recipe:..

INGREDIENTS:..

....

....

DIRECTIONS:..

....

....

....

....

YIELD:..

Recipe:..

INGREDIENTS:..

....

....

DIRECTIONS:..

....

....

....

....

YIELD:..

Recipe:..

INGREDIENTS:..

....

....

DIRECTIONS:..

....

....

....

....

YIELD:..

Three Breads a-Rising

Christmas day is a day of joy and charity.
May God make you very rich in both.

PHILLIPS BROOKS

You, Lord, are the giver of life and all the joys it contains. Thank You for each breath we take, each thought we think, and for providing all that is needed to live each day with You. Amen.

This is what God told us: God has given us eternal life, and this life is in his Son.

1 JOHN 5:11 NCV

Nutty Pumpkin Bread *

3½ cups flour

2 teaspoons salt

1 teaspoon nutmeg

1 teaspoon cinnamon

3 cups sugar

2 teaspoons baking soda

2 cups canned pumpkin

4 eggs, beaten

½ cup vegetable oil

½ cup butter, melted

1 cup milk

Preheat oven to 350 degrees. In large bowl, combine flour, salt, nutmeg, cinnamon, sugar, and baking soda. In separate bowl, beat together pumpkin, eggs, oil, butter, and milk. Blend in flour mixture thoroughly and pour into 3 greased and floured standard loaf pans, filling each ⅔ full. Bake for 45 to 60 minutes.

YIELD: 3 STANDARD LOAVES

Nutty Upside-Down Pineapple Muffins *

¼ cup packed brown sugar

2 tablespoons butter, melted

12 pecan halves

1½ cups bran flakes

1 (8 ounce) can crushed pineapple

¼ cup milk

1 egg

¼ cup vegetable oil

½ cup coarsely chopped pecans

1¼ cups flour

3½ teaspoons baking powder

1 teaspoon salt

⅓ cup sugar

Preheat oven to 400 degrees. Cream brown sugar and butter. Using teaspoon, spoon mixture into greased 12-cup muffin pan. Place pecan half in each. Mix together bran flakes, pineapple, and milk. Let stand for 2 minutes. Beat in egg and oil. Add chopped pecans. Combine remaining dry ingredients. Add to wet mixture and stir until blended. Spoon into muffin cups. Bake for 25 minutes.

Yield: 12 muffins

Aunt Sandy's Blackberry Bread *

3 cups flour

2 cups sugar

2½ teaspoons cinnamon

1 teaspoon baking soda

1 teaspoon salt

1 cup vegetable oil

¼ cup milk

4 eggs

2 cups fresh blackberries

Preheat oven to 350 degrees. Sift together dry ingredients in medium mixing bowl, forming a well in center of mixture. Add oil, milk, eggs, and blackberries. Stir until mixture is moistened. Divide dough in half and place each half in greased and floured standard loaf pan. Bake for 55 minutes.

YIELD: 2 STANDARD LOAVES

Butterlove Rolls *

1 package yeast

½ cup warm water

½ cup milk

1 egg, beaten

1 teaspoon salt

½ cup sugar

2½ cups flour

¼ cup butter, melted and divided

Preheat oven to 400 degrees. Dissolve yeast in water; set aside. In saucepan, scald milk. Cool in large bowl. Add egg, salt, sugar, and yeast mixture. Mix well. Add flour. Mix and knead gently. Let rise until double in size. Roll out in two circles and brush with half of butter. Cut into pie-shaped wedges and roll up crescent-roll style. Brush with remaining butter. Let rise. Bake for 15 minutes or until golden brown.

YIELD: 12 ROLLS

Dasher's Cheddar-Garlic Biscuits

2½ cups flour

1 tablespoon baking powder

½ teaspoon baking soda

½ teaspoon salt

2 tablespoons shortening

1 cup buttermilk

¼ cup butter, melted

½ cup shredded cheddar cheese

½ teaspoon garlic powder

2 tablespoons butter, melted

½ teaspoon garlic-herb powder

Preheat oven to 400 degrees. In large bowl, combine flour, baking powder, baking soda, and salt. Stir well. Cut in shortening with pastry blender. Add buttermilk and melted butter. Stir until dry ingredients are moistened. Add cheese and garlic powder. Stir gently to combine. Drop by spoonful onto ungreased cookie sheet. Brush with 2 tablespoons butter and sprinkle lightly with garlic-herb powder. Bake for 15 minutes or until lightly browned.

Yield: 2 dozen biscuits

Cranberry Cobblescones

2 cups flour

4 teaspoons baking powder

½ teaspoon salt

3 tablespoons sugar, divided

¼ cup butter

2 eggs

½ cup light cream

¾ cup cranberry sauce

½ cup shredded apple

2 tablespoons brown sugar

½ teaspoon cinnamon

1 tablespoon milk

Preheat oven to 450 degrees. In large bowl, combine flour, baking powder, salt, and 1 tablespoon sugar. With pastry blender, cut in butter until particles are fine. Add eggs and cream. Stir until dry ingredients are moistened. Roll out to 16x8-inch rectangle. In separate bowl, combine cranberry sauce, apple, brown sugar, and cinnamon. Spread out over half of dough. Fold dough over filling. Seal edges. Brush with milk and sprinkle with remaining 2 tablespoons sugar. Transfer to ungreased cookie sheet and cut into squares. Bake for 18 minutes or until golden brown.

YIELD: 15 SQUARES

Christmas Surprise Muffins

2 cups flour

¼ cup sugar

½ teaspoon salt

1 tablespoon baking powder

¼ cup shortening, melted and cooled slightly

1 egg

1 cup milk

4 tablespoons strawberry jam

Preheat oven to 425 degrees. Line 12-cup muffin pan. In medium bowl, combine flour, sugar, salt, and baking powder. Mix well. Add shortening, egg, and milk. Stir just until blended. Fill muffin cups half full. Spoon 1 teaspoon strawberry jam onto center of batter. Add additional batter to fill cups ¾ full. Bake for 25 minutes.

YIELD: 12 MUFFINS

Applesauce Nut Bread

2 cups flour

¾ cup sugar

3 tablespoons baking powder

1½ teaspoons salt

½ teaspoon baking soda

½ teaspoon cinnamon

1 egg, beaten

1 cup applesauce

1 tablespoon shortening, melted

1 cup chopped walnuts

Preheat oven to 350 degrees. Sift together flour, sugar, baking powder, salt, baking soda, and cinnamon. In large mixing bowl, combine egg, applesauce, and shortening. Mix well. Add dry ingredients. Combine until moistened. Stir in walnuts. Pour into greased standard loaf pan. Bake for 1 hour.

YIELD: 1 STANDARD LOAF

North Pole Gingerbread

½ cup butter, softened

½ cup brown sugar

1 cup dark molasses

1 teaspoon cinnamon

2 teaspoons ginger

¼ teaspoon cloves

2 eggs

2½ cups flour

2 teaspoons baking soda

1 cup boiling water

Preheat oven to 350 degrees. In large bowl, cream together butter and brown sugar. Add molasses and combine well. Stir in cinnamon, ginger, and cloves. Add eggs. Stir well. Add flour and mix well. Put baking soda into boiling water. Add to creamed mixture. Batter will be thin. Pour into greased 8x8-inch pan. Bake for 50 minutes.

Yield: 9 servings

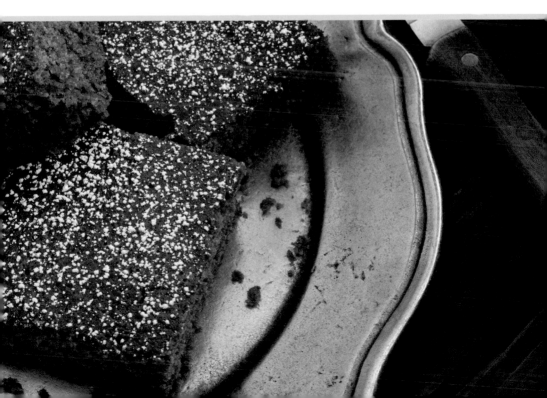

Christmas in Hawaii Bread

3 eggs

2 cups sugar

1 cup vegetable oil

2 teaspoons vanilla

2 cups grated zucchini

3 cups flour

1 teaspoon baking powder

1 teaspoon salt

1 teaspoon baking soda

1 cup crushed pineapple, drained

½ cup raisins

1 cup chopped pecans or walnuts

3 teaspoons cinnamon

Preheat oven to 325 degrees. In large bowl, beat eggs, sugar, oil, and vanilla until creamed. Add zucchini. In separate bowl, sift together flour, baking powder, salt, and baking soda. Add to egg and sugar mixture. Stir in pineapple, raisins, nuts, and cinnamon. Mix well. Pour into 2 greased standard loaf pans. Bake for 1 hour.

YIELD: 2 STANDARD LOAVES

Rudolph's Mincemeat Bread

3 cups flour

3½ teaspoons baking powder

¼ teaspoon baking soda

½ teaspoon salt

¾ cup packed brown sugar

1½ cups chopped walnuts

2 eggs

½ cup milk

⅓ cup vegetable oil

1 cup prepared mincemeat

Preheat oven to 350 degrees. In large bowl, sift together flour, baking powder, baking soda, and salt. Stir in brown sugar and walnuts; set aside. In small bowl, beat eggs. Add milk, oil, and mincemeat. Mix well. Add to flour mixture and stir until evenly moist. Spoon into greased standard loaf pan. Spread top evenly. Bake for 1 hour.

YIELD: 1 STANDARD LOAF

Nana's Sweet Potato Bread

3½ cups flour

3 cups sugar

2 teaspoons baking soda

1½ teaspoons salt

1 teaspoon cinnamon

1 teaspoon nutmeg

1 cup vegetable oil

2 cups cooked, mashed sweet potato

¾ cup water

4 eggs

Preheat oven to 350 degrees. Sift together flour, sugar, baking soda, salt, cinnamon, and nutmeg. Add oil, sweet potato, water, and eggs. Mix well. Grease and flour two 1-pound coffee cans. Divide batter and fill cans half full. Bake for 70 minutes.

YIELD: 2 LOAVES

Christmas Carrot Bread

2 cups flour

1½ cups sugar

2 teaspoons baking soda

2 teaspoons cinnamon

½ teaspoon salt

½ cup dried currants or raisins

½ cup sweetened flaked coconut

½ cup chopped pecans

¾ cup vegetable oil

2 teaspoons vanilla

2 cups grated raw carrot

3 eggs, beaten

Preheat oven to 350 degrees. In large bowl, sift together flour, sugar, baking soda, cinnamon, and salt. Add currants, coconut, pecans, oil, vanilla, carrot, and eggs. Mix well with electric mixer but don't overmix. Pour into 2 greased standard loaf pans. Bake for 60 minutes.

YIELD: 2 STANDARD LOAVES

Peachy Muffins

1 egg

½ cup milk

¼ cup vegetable oil

1½ cups flour

½ cup sugar

2 teaspoons baking powder

½ teaspoon salt

½ teaspoon cinnamon

½ cup peeled and chopped peaches

Preheat oven to 400 degrees. In large bowl, beat egg. Stir in milk and oil. In separate bowl, sift together flour, sugar, baking powder, salt, and cinnamon. Add to milk mixture, beating until dry ingredients are moistened. Fold in peaches. Do not overmix. Line 12-cup muffin pan. Fill cups to ⅔ full. Bake for 25 minutes.

YIELD: 12 MUFFINS

Banana Orange Bread

½ cup butter, softened

1⅓ cups sugar

2 eggs

3 large bananas, mashed

½ teaspoon grated orange rind

1½ teaspoons orange juice

2 cups flour

1 teaspoon baking soda

2 teaspoons baking powder

¼ teaspoon salt

½ cup chopped pecans

Preheat oven to 350 degrees. In large bowl, cream butter and sugar until fluffy. Add eggs. Beat well. In separate bowl, combine bananas, orange rind, and orange juice. In another bowl, sift together flour, baking soda, baking powder, and salt. Add to creamed mixture alternately with banana mixture. Stir in pecans. Pour into greased standard loaf pan. Bake for 70 minutes.

YIELD: 1 STANDARD LOAF

Baked Apple Bread

4 cups peeled, chopped apples

2 cups sugar

1 cup chopped pecans

3 cups flour

2 teaspoons baking soda

¾ teaspoon cinnamon

¼ teaspoon nutmeg

¼ teaspoon cloves

¼ teaspoon salt

1 cup butter, melted

2 teaspoons vanilla

2 eggs, beaten

In large bowl, combine apples, sugar, and pecans. Mix well and let stand for 1 hour, stirring frequently. In separate bowl, sift together flour, baking soda, spices, and salt. Add to apple mixture. Stir in butter, vanilla, and eggs. Mix well. Spoon batter into 2 greased and floured standard loaf pans. Bake for 75 minutes.

YIELD: 2 STANDARD LOAVES

Christmas Morning Casserole Bread

4 cups flour

1¼ teaspoons salt

1½ teaspoons baking soda

¾ cup packed dark brown sugar

1¼ cups raisins

2 tablespoons butter, melted

2 eggs, slightly beaten

1½ cups buttermilk

Preheat oven to 350 degrees. In large bowl, combine flour, salt, baking soda, brown sugar, and raisins. Add butter, eggs, and buttermilk. Mix only until dry ingredients are moistened. Spoon into 2 greased 1-quart casserole dishes. Bake for 45 minutes. Turn out onto rack to cool.

YIELD: 2 LOAVES

Jellied Cranberry Muffins

1¾ cups flour

¼ cup sugar

2½ teaspoons baking powder

¾ teaspoon salt

1 egg, well beaten

¾ cup milk

⅓ cup vegetable oil

1 (8 ounce) can jellied cranberry sauce, chilled

Preheat oven to 400 degrees. In large bowl, combine flour, sugar, baking powder, and salt. Make a well in center of dry ingredients. Combine egg, milk, and oil in small bowl. Add to dry ingredients. Mix until dry ingredients are moistened. In separate bowl, cut cranberry sauce into ½-inch cubes. Line 12-cup muffin pan. Fill each cup ⅓ full. Place 2 to 3 cubes over batter in each cup. Top with remaining batter. Bake for 25 minutes.

YIELD: 12 MUFFINS

Cornmeal Ham Muffins

1 cup flour

2 teaspoons baking powder

1 teaspoon sugar

⅛ teaspoon salt

¼ cup cornmeal

2 eggs

¼ cup olive oil

1 cup milk

¼ cup ground cooked ham

Preheat oven to 400 degrees. In medium bowl, sift together flour, baking powder, sugar, and salt. Add cornmeal and mix well. Set aside. In medium bowl, beat together eggs, oil, and milk. Add flour mixture and ham to egg mixture, stirring until just moistened. Spoon batter into 8 standard muffin pan cups with greased bottoms. Bake for 18 minutes.

Yield: 8 muffins

My Favorite Christmas Bread Recipes

Recipe:

INGREDIENTS:

DIRECTIONS:

YIELD:

Recipe:

INGREDIENTS:

DIRECTIONS:

YIELD:

Recipe:..
INGREDIENTS:.....................................
....
....
DIRECTIONS:......................................
....
....
....
....
YIELD:...

Recipe:..
INGREDIENTS:.....................................
....
....
DIRECTIONS:......................................
....
....
....
....
YIELD:...

Recipe:..
INGREDIENTS:.....................................
....
....
DIRECTIONS:......................................
....
....
....
....
YIELD:...

On the fourth day of Christmas my true love sent to me:

Four Breakfast Dishes a-Baking

Love is what's in the room with you at Christmas
if you stop opening presents and listen.

Author Unknown

Father in heaven, help us keep our minds about us as we celebrate the Christmas season, ever aware of and grateful for the hope and mercy You have poured out on us. Amen.

May all who come to you be glad and joyful. May all who are thankful for your salvation always say, "How great is God!"

PSALM 70:4 GNT

Matchless Coconut Almond Granola *

8 cups old-fashioned rolled oats

1 cup slivered or sliced almonds

1 cup unsweetened coconut shavings

½ cup raw sesame seeds

½ cup raw pumpkin seeds

½ cup raw sunflower seeds

¾ cup pure maple syrup

½ cup coconut oil, melted

¼ cup honey

1 tablespoon molasses

1 tablespoon vanilla

2 teaspoons cinnamon

1 teaspoon sea salt

Preheat oven to 350 degrees. Combine oats, almonds, coconut, and seeds in large mixing bowl. In separate bowl, stir together remaining ingredients; pour over dry ingredients. Mix well. Line two large rimmed baking sheets with parchment paper. Pour half of granola onto each sheet and spread evenly. Bake for 12 minutes, toss granola gently, and reduce heat to 325 degrees. Continue baking 30 minutes longer, stirring every 10 minutes. Cool on cookie sheets and store in airtight containers.

YIELD: 10 CUPS

Elegant Shrimp Scramble *

3 slices bacon

¾ cup chopped green bell pepper

½ cup chopped onion

¼ teaspoon salt

¼ teaspoon cayenne pepper

10 ounces cooked shrimp, coarsely chopped

6 eggs, beaten

¼ cup light cream

½ teaspoon Worcestershire sauce

Cook and crumble bacon; set aside, reserving drippings. Sauté bell pepper and onion in reserved bacon drippings until tender. Add salt and cayenne pepper. Add shrimp. Stir until heated thoroughly. In bowl, combine eggs, cream, Worcestershire, and bacon. Add to shrimp mixture and cook until eggs are firm, stirring occasionally.

YIELD: 6 SERVINGS

Peach Waffles *

⅓ cup shortening

½ cup sugar

2 eggs

2 cups flour

1 tablespoon baking powder

½ teaspoon salt

1 cup milk

1½ cups peeled, diced peaches

½ teaspoon lemon juice

½ teaspoon vanilla

1 tablespoon powdered sugar

In large bowl, cream shortening, gradually adding sugar. Beat well with electric mixer on low speed. Add eggs, one at a time, beating well after each addition. Set aside. In medium bowl, combine flour, baking powder, and salt. Add to creamed mixture alternately with milk. Stir in peaches, lemon juice, and vanilla. Bake on preheated, oiled waffle iron. Sprinkle with powdered sugar before serving.

YIELD: 16 WAFFLES

Toasted Crab Delight

4 slices tomato

½ pound crabmeat

2 English muffins, split, toasted, and buttered

½ cup mayonnaise

¼ cup chili sauce

1 tablespoon lemon juice

1 tablespoon Worcestershire sauce

4 slices bacon, cooked and crumbled

1 egg, hard cooked and coarsely chopped

Place 1 tomato slice and ¼ crabmeat on each English muffin half. In small bowl, combine mayonnaise, chili sauce, lemon juice, and Worcestershire. Pour over crabmeat. Top with bacon and egg.

YIELD: 2 SERVINGS

Elegant Pear Coffee Cake

1 (29 ounce) can pear halves

½ cup butter, softened

½ cup sugar

3 eggs

1¾ cups flour

2 teaspoons baking powder

1 teaspoon salt

1 teaspoon grated lemon rind

⅓ cup milk

1 cup sour cream

2 tablespoons brown sugar

1 tablespoon grated lemon rind

Preheat oven to 350 degrees. Drain and slice pears. Set aside. In large bowl, cream butter with sugar until fluffy. Add eggs and beat well. In separate bowl, sift together flour, baking powder, and salt. In measuring cup, add 1 teaspoon lemon rind to milk. Alternately add milk mixture and dry ingredients to butter mixture. Pour into buttered 10x8-inch baking pan. Arrange pear slices in rows on top. Combine sour cream, brown sugar, and remaining tablespoon lemon rind. Spoon over pears. Bake for 45 minutes.

YIELD: 9 SERVINGS

Ham and Cheese Quiche

2 eggs, beaten

⅓ cup mayonnaise

⅓ cup evaporated milk

2 tablespoons flour

½ teaspoon dry mustard

2 tablespoons chopped onion

½ cup shredded cheddar cheese

1 cup shredded swiss cheese

1 (6 ounce) container fresh ham salad

1 prepared (8 inch) piecrust

Preheat oven to 325 degrees. In large bowl, mix together eggs, mayonnaise, milk, flour, mustard, onion, cheeses, and ham salad. Pour into piecrust. Bake for 45 minutes.

YIELD: 6 SERVINGS

Christmas Day Coffee Cake

2 cups flour

2 teaspoons instant coffee granules

2 cups packed brown sugar

1 teaspoon cinnamon

½ teaspoon salt

¼ teaspoon nutmeg

½ cup butter

1 (8 ounce) carton sour cream

1 teaspoon baking soda

1 egg, beaten

½ cup chopped pecans or walnuts

Preheat oven to 350 degrees. In large bowl, combine flour and coffee granules. Add brown sugar, cinnamon, salt, and nutmeg. Stir well. Cut in butter with pastry blender until mixture resembles coarse meal. Press half of crumb mixture into greased 9x9-inch baking pan. Set aside. Combine sour cream and baking soda, stirring well. Add to remaining crumb mixture. Stir until dry ingredients are moistened. Add egg. Stir gently to combine. Pour sour cream mixture over crumb mixture in pan. Sprinkle with nuts. Bake for 45 minutes.

YIELD: 10 SERVINGS

Easy Eggs Florentine

¼ cup butter, melted

¼ cup flour

½ teaspoon salt

¼ teaspoon pepper

2 cups milk

2 (10 ounce) packages frozen chopped spinach, cooked and drained

1 tablespoon lemon juice

12 eggs, poached or sunny side up

½ cup grated Parmesan cheese

In medium saucepan, combine butter, flour, salt, and pepper over low heat. Cook, stirring constantly, until smooth and bubbly. Add milk and cook, stirring constantly, until mixture thickens. Remove from heat and set aside. Combine spinach and lemon juice; spread in 2-quart baking dish. Arrange eggs on top of spinach. Pour white sauce over eggs. Sprinkle with cheese. Broil 6 inches from heat for 3 to 5 minutes or until lightly browned and bubbly. Serve hot.

YIELD: 6 SERVINGS

Santa's Reward Baked Omelet

6 slices bacon

1 medium onion, chopped

8 eggs, lightly beaten

1 cup milk

1 tablespoon chopped parsley

½ teaspoon salt

¼ teaspoon pepper

1 cup shredded cheddar cheese

1 cup shredded swiss cheese

1 tablespoon flour

Preheat oven to 350 degrees. Fry bacon and crumble, reserving 1 tablespoon drippings. Sauté onion in bacon drippings until tender. Add bacon, eggs, milk, parsley, salt, and pepper. Mix well. Combine cheeses and flour. Add to egg mixture. Pour into 1½-quart casserole dish. Bake for 40 minutes. Serve immediately.

YIELD: 6 SERVINGS

Early Morning Hamwiches

2 tablespoons chopped onion

1 tablespoon chopped green bell pepper

1 tablespoon butter, melted

6 eggs, beaten

1½ cups shredded cheddar cheese, divided

½ cup finely chopped cooked ham

¼ teaspoon salt

¼ teaspoon pepper

6 buns, toasted and buttered

Sauté onion and bell pepper in butter until tender. In medium bowl, combine onion mixture with eggs, 1 cup cheese, ham, salt, and pepper. Shape into 6 patties and cook on buttered, preheated griddle until eggs are set. Turn and cook on other side. Sprinkle with remaining cheese. Serve on warm buns.

YIELD: 6 HAMWICHES

Oven-Baked Sausage and Pancakes

2 eggs

1 cup milk

1¼ cups flour

1 tablespoon baking powder

1 tablespoon sugar

½ teaspoon salt

2 tablespoons shortening, melted

2 (8 ounce) packages precooked sausage links

Butter and syrup

Preheat oven to 450 degrees. In large bowl, beat eggs until light and fluffy. Add milk and stir. In separate bowl, combine flour, baking powder, sugar, and salt. Add to egg mixture. Add shortening. Beat until batter is smooth. Pour into 2 greased 8-inch round cake pans. Arrange sausage links on batter like spokes on a wheel. Bake for 15 minutes. Cut each pancake into 5 wedges. Serve hot with butter and syrup.

YIELD: 8 SERVINGS

Fancy Baked Grapefruit

2 grapefruit

2 tablespoons chopped raisins or figs

2 tablespoons chopped walnuts

3 tablespoons honey

Preheat oven to 300 degrees. Cut grapefruit in half crosswise. Run knife around each segment to loosen. Combine raisins and walnuts. Place in center of each grapefruit half. Drizzle with honey. Bake for 12 minutes or until heated through. Serve immediately.

YIELD: 4 SERVINGS

Blitzen's Egg and Bacon Bake

¼ cup dry bread crumbs

1 tablespoon butter, melted

5 hard-boiled eggs, sliced

3 slices bacon, cut up, fried crisp, and drained

1 cup sour cream

3 tablespoons finely chopped onion

1 tablespoon milk

½ teaspoon salt

¼ teaspoon paprika

¼ teaspoon pepper

½ cup shredded cheddar cheese

Preheat oven to 350 degrees. Toss bread crumbs with butter. Divide among 4 buttered 10-ounce custard cups. Layer egg slices over bread crumbs. In medium bowl, mix together bacon, sour cream, onion, milk, salt, paprika, and pepper. Spoon onto eggs. Top with cheese. Bake, uncovered, for 12 minutes.

YIELD: 4 SERVINGS

Cheesy French Bread Bake

½ (1 pound) loaf french bread

2 cups shredded Muenster or Monterey Jack cheese

¼ pound prosciutto or fully cooked ham, finely chopped

4 green onions with tops, sliced

4 eggs, slightly beaten

1½ cups milk

½ cup dry white wine or water

1 tablespoon Dijon-style mustard

1 teaspoon red pepper sauce

2 tablespoons grated Parmesan cheese

Preheat oven to 325 degrees. Cut bread into 16 slices. Arrange 8 slices in ungreased 11x7x2-inch baking dish. Top with cheese, prosciutto, and onions. Arrange remaining bread on top. Combine eggs, milk, wine, mustard, and pepper sauce. Mix well. Pour over bread. Sprinkle with Parmesan cheese. Bake, uncovered, for about 75 minutes. Let stand for 10 minutes before cutting.

YIELD: 8 SERVINGS

Cupid's Corn Toast

1 cup cornmeal

2 eggs

¼ teaspoon salt

1¼ cups evaporated milk

3 tablespoons butter

8 slices day-old white bread

½ stick (4 tablespoons) butter

1 cup maple syrup, warmed

Place cornmeal in pie pan. In medium bowl, beat eggs. Stir in salt and milk. In large skillet, melt 3 tablespoons butter. Dip bread in egg mixture. Turn once and let stand until bread is moist but not falling apart. Place in cornmeal, turning to coat both sides. Cook in hot butter until brown. Turn and brown on other side. Add butter if needed to keep skillet greased. Serve with remaining ½ stick butter and syrup.

YIELD: 8 SERVINGS

Royal Fruit and Berries

¼ cup honey

Juice of 1 lime

1 ripe mango, peeled and diced

½ pint fresh blueberries

½ pint fresh raspberries

2 kiwi, peeled, sliced into rounds, and quartered

In small saucepan, heat honey and lime juice until honey is melted. In medium serving bowl, combine mango, berries, and kiwi. Pour honey mixture over fruit and berries. Let stand for at least 5 minutes before serving.

YIELD: 4 CUPS

Cheesy Herb Omelets

4 eggs

2 tablespoons light cream

2 tablespoons chopped fresh chives

¼ teaspoon salt

¼ teaspoon pepper

1 tablespoon butter

6 tablespoons shredded swiss cheese

4 tablespoons shredded cheddar cheese

1 tablespoon grated Parmesan cheese

Whip together eggs, cream, chives, salt, and pepper, fully incorporating egg whites. In large nonstick skillet, melt butter over high heat until bubbly. Pour egg mixture into skillet. Use spatula to pull from sides of skillet until eggs are no longer runny but still moist. Add cheeses on top. Fold over and slide onto plate. Let rest for 1 minute before serving.

YIELD: 2 OMELETS

Scrambled Eggs and Sausage Balls

1 pound pork sausage

1½ cups biscuit mix

1 cup shredded cheddar cheese

6 eggs

2 tablespoons milk

¼ teaspoon salt

¼ teaspoon pepper

1 tablespoon butter

Preheat oven to 400 degrees. Combine sausage, biscuit mix, and cheese. Mix thoroughly. Roll into balls. Place on cookie sheet and bake for 15 minutes. With wire whisk, beat together eggs, milk, salt, and pepper. When sausage balls have 5 minutes left to cook, melt butter in nonstick skillet on medium heat. Add egg mixture. Use spatula to pull from sides of skillet until eggs are no longer runny but still moist. Serve immediately.

YIELD: 4 SERVINGS

My Favorite Christmas Breakfast Recipes

Recipe: ....

INGREDIENTS: ....
....
....

DIRECTIONS: ....
....
....
....
....

YIELD: ....

Recipe: ....

INGREDIENTS: ....
....
....

DIRECTIONS: ....
....
....
....
....

YIELD: ....

Recipe:

INGREDIENTS:

DIRECTIONS:

YIELD:

Recipe:

INGREDIENTS:

DIRECTIONS:

YIELD:

Recipe:

INGREDIENTS:

DIRECTIONS:

YIELD:

On the fifth day of Christmas my true love sent to me:

Five Candies a-Dancing

Christmas should make us remember the poor and
the needy; for a charitable deed is the best close of any
chapter of our lives, and the best promise too.

ALEXANDER SMITH

How amazing, Father, to think back on a year gone by and remember Your comfort, Your strength, Your loving-kindness, Your tender ministrations. And what hope it brings to look forward to another year with You. Amen.

Thank God for his gift that is too wonderful for words!

2 Corinthians 9:15 cev

Pecan Pralines *

3 cups sugar

1 cup milk

2 tablespoons light corn syrup

1 teaspoon salt

1 tablespoon butter

1 teaspoon vanilla

3 cups pecan halves

In large saucepan, cook sugar, milk, corn syrup, and salt to soft-ball stage (235 degrees). Remove from heat. Add butter and vanilla, stirring mixture for 1 or 2 minutes or until very slightly opaque. Quickly add pecans to mixture and stir. Drop immediately onto waxed paper and allow to set.

YIELD: 25 PRALINES

Pecan Turtles *

24 soft caramels

2 tablespoons evaporated milk

16 ounces milk chocolate chips

1½ cups pecan halves

½ teaspoon sea salt

Melt caramels in milk in bowl placed over simmering pan of water, stirring constantly. Remove from heat. While caramel mixture cools slightly, melt chocolate chips. Spoon chocolate into little puddles on waxed paper. Before it sets, sink three pecan halves into edges of each chocolate puddle for "turtle's head and feet." Spoon thickened caramel mixture into center and cover with more chocolate, leaving turtle's head and feet sticking out slightly. Sprinkle with salt.

YIELD: 2 DOZEN TURTLES

Granny C's Crazy Crunch *

2 quarts popped popcorn

1⅓ cups nuts

1⅓ cups sugar

1 cup butter

½ cup light corn syrup

1 teaspoon vanilla

Spread out popcorn and nuts on buttered, rimmed cookie sheet. In medium saucepan, combine sugar, butter, and corn syrup. Bring to boil over medium heat, stirring constantly. Boil, stirring occasionally, for 10 to 15 minutes or until mixture is light caramel color. Remove from heat. Stir in vanilla. Pour over popcorn and nuts. Mix to coat. Spread to dry. Break apart and store in airtight container.

YIELD: 2 POUNDS

Angel Sweets

1 cup semisweet chocolate chips

2 tablespoons butter

1 egg

1 cup sifted powdered sugar

1 cup chopped walnuts

2 cups miniature marshmallows

½ cup sweetened flaked coconut

In medium saucepan, melt chocolate and butter over low heat. Remove from heat and blend in egg. Stir in powdered sugar, walnuts, and marshmallows, blending well. Shape into 1-inch balls. Roll in coconut. Chill.

YIELD: 48 BALLS

Potato Kisses

⅔ cup hot mashed potato

2 teaspoons butter, melted

3½ cups powdered sugar

2½ tablespoons cocoa or 1½ squares
baking chocolate, melted

1 teaspoon vanilla

⅛ teaspoon salt

½ pound sweetened flaked coconut

Put mashed potato through ricer or sieve to remove lumps. In medium bowl, combine potatoes and butter. Beat until well blended. Add powdered sugar and beat until thoroughly blended. Add cocoa (if using melted chocolate, cool first). Beat thoroughly. Mix in vanilla, salt, and coconut. Drop by teaspoonful onto waxed paper. Chill until hardened. Store in tightly covered container.

YIELD: 1½ POUNDS

Santa's Sponge Candy

1 cup sugar

1 cup dark corn syrup

1 tablespoon cider vinegar

1 tablespoon baking soda

In heavy 2-quart saucepan, heat sugar, corn syrup, and vinegar to boiling over medium heat, stirring constantly. When sugar is dissolved, stop stirring and bring to boil. Continue to boil until mixture reaches hard crack stage (300 degrees). Remove from heat. Quickly stir in baking soda thoroughly. Pour mixture into ungreased 13x9-inch pan. Do not spread. Cool thoroughly. Break into pieces.

YIELD: 3 DOZEN PIECES

Candied Fruit Roll

½ pound raisins

¼ pound dried figs

¼ pound dried apricots

½ pound dates

¼ pound candied pineapple

½ pound sweetened flaked coconut

½ pound pecans or walnuts, coarsely chopped

3 tablespoons butter, melted

2 cups sugar

¾ cup water

3 tablespoons vinegar

Wash raisins, figs, apricots, and dates. Pat dry and remove any seeds or pits. Put fruit, candied pineapple, and coconut through food grinder, using coarse blade. In large bowl, combine fruit mixture with nuts. Coat bottom and sides of rimmed cookie sheet with melted butter. Spread fruit and nut mixture evenly. In 3-quart saucepan, combine sugar, water, and vinegar. Mix well. Boil without stirring to soft-ball stage (235 degrees). Without scraping sides, pour syrup over fruit. Let cool. Knead mixture until well mixed. Form into 2 rolls about 2 inches in diameter. Wrap in waxed paper. Chill for 3 hours. Cut into ¼-inch slices.

YIELD: 3½ POUNDS

Almond Butter Crunch

1 cup sugar

1 cup butter

2 tablespoons water

1 tablespoon light corn syrup

¾ cup chopped toasted almonds

½ cup semisweet chocolate chips

Butter 9x9-inch baking pan. In heavy 2-quart saucepan, heat sugar, butter, water, and corn syrup to boiling over medium heat, stirring constantly. Continuing to stir, cook for about 12 minutes (290 degrees). Mixture will be light brown and thickened. Remove from heat. Stir in almonds. Spread evenly in baking pan. Sprinkle with chocolate chips. When chocolate is softened, carefully spread over candy. Let stand until firm (about 3 hours). Remove from pan and break into pieces. Cover and refrigerate.

YIELD: 6 DOZEN PIECES

Christmas Bonbons

1 cup butter, melted

1 (14 ounce) can sweetened
condensed milk

1 teaspoon vanilla

8 cups powdered sugar

2 cups sweetened flaked coconut

2 cups pecans, chopped

16 ounces molding chocolate

In large bowl, combine butter, milk, vanilla, powdered sugar, coconut, and pecans. Shape dough into balls and chill for 2 hours. Melt molding chocolate. Dip balls into chocolate and place on waxed paper.

YIELD: 60 BALLS

Chocolate-Cherry Mash

2 cups sugar

⅔ cup evaporated milk

⅛ teaspoon salt

12 large marshmallows

½ cup butter

1 (6 ounce) package cherry chips

1 teaspoon vanilla

1 (12 ounce) package chocolate chips

¾ cup peanut butter

6 ounces peanuts, crushed

In large saucepan, combine sugar, milk, salt, marshmallows, and butter. Boil over medium heat for 5 minutes, stirring constantly. Remove from heat. Stir in cherry chips and vanilla. Pour into greased 13x9-inch pan. In double boiler, combine chocolate chips and peanut butter. When melted and well blended, add crushed peanuts. Pour over cherry mixture and chill. Cut into small squares. Store in refrigerator.

YIELD: 20 SQUARES

Sugarplum Candies

2 cups pitted prunes, finely chopped

2 cups raisins

1⅓ cups finely chopped walnuts

2 cups sugar

½ cup light corn syrup

½ cup water

½ teaspoon vanilla

¼ teaspoon salt

1 cup sweetened flaked coconut, finely chopped

Combine prunes, raisins, and walnuts. Stir well. In heavy 2-quart saucepan, combine sugar, corn syrup, and water. Cook over low heat, stirring gently until sugar dissolves. Cover and cook over medium heat for 3 minutes. Uncover and cook until mixture reaches soft-ball stage (235 degrees). Remove from heat. Cool for 10 minutes. Pour sugar mixture into large mixing bowl. Add vanilla and salt. Beat on high speed for 5 minutes or until fluffy. Stir in prune mixture. Press into lightly greased 9x9-inch baking pan. Chill for 1 hour. Cut into 64 squares. Make into balls and roll in coconut. Store in airtight container.

YIELD: 64 SUGARPLUMS

Sour Cream Glazed Pecans

3 cups sugar

1 (8 ounce) carton sour cream

2 teaspoons vanilla

5 cups pecan halves

In heavy 2½-quart saucepan, combine sugar and sour cream. Cook over low heat, stirring constantly, until mixture reaches soft-ball stage (235 degrees). Remove from heat and stir in vanilla. Continue to stir until mixture begins to cool. Add pecan halves and stir well. Spread on single layer of waxed paper. Cool completely.

YIELD: 6 CUPS

Coconut Date Balls

½ cup butter

¾ cup sugar

1 tablespoon milk

⅛ teaspoon salt

1 egg

½ teaspoon vanilla

1 cup chopped dates

2 cups rice cereal

½ cup sweetened flaked coconut, finely chopped

In heavy saucepan, combine butter, sugar, milk, salt, and egg. Over medium heat, stir constantly until mixture comes to boil (about 2 minutes). Remove from heat. Add vanilla, dates, and rice cereal. Mix well. Shape into 1-inch balls and roll in coconut.

Yield: 40 balls

Holiday Divinity

3 cups sugar

¾ cup light corn syrup

¼ teaspoon salt

¾ cup water

2 egg whites

1 (3 ounce) package strawberry gelatin

In heavy saucepan, combine sugar, corn syrup, salt, and water. Stirring constantly, cook until mixture boils. Without stirring, continue to cook until mixture reaches hard-ball stage (250 degrees). In small bowl, beat egg whites to soft peaks. Add gelatin and beat at high speed until mixture begins to lose gloss. Fold into sugar mixture. Drop by spoonful onto waxed paper.

YIELD: 30 PIECES

Comet's Clusters

1 (24 ounce) package almond bark, melted

1 cup pecans, peanuts, or walnuts

1 cup chow mein noodles

2 cups miniature marshmallows

4 cups popped popcorn, lightly salted

1 cup rice cereal

In large bowl, combine almond bark, nuts, noodles, marshmallows, popcorn, and rice cereal. Drop by tablespoonful onto waxed paper.

YIELD: 48 PIECES

Vixen's Royal Fudge

4½ cups sugar

3 tablespoons butter

1 (12 ounce) package milk chocolate chips

3 (4 ounce) packages German chocolate chips

1 pint marshmallow crème

⅛ teaspoon salt

1 (14 ounce) can sweetened condensed milk

2 cups English walnuts

In large heavy saucepan, combine sugar, butter, and chocolate chips. Cook over medium heat, stirring constantly, until mixture comes to full boil. Continue to boil for 6 minutes (exactly). Remove from heat and stir in marshmallow crème, salt, milk, and walnuts. Pour into 8x8-inch baking pan. When set, cut into small squares.

YIELD: 25 PIECES

Graham Cracker Surprises

18 graham crackers, broken in half

1 cup butter

1 cup packed dark brown sugar

1 cup chopped mixed nuts

Preheat oven to 375 degrees. Place graham crackers on parchment-lined cookie sheet in one layer. In saucepan, melt butter and brown sugar. Bring mixture to boil and boil for 2 minutes. Sprinkle nuts over graham crackers. Pour butter mixture over nuts and bake for 10 minutes. Cool thoroughly before breaking into pieces.

YIELD: 3 DOZEN PIECES

Chocolate Gingerbread Fudge

1 (12 ounce) package German chocolate chips, melted

1 (12 ounce) package white chocolate chips, melted

2 cups sweetened condensed milk

1½ teaspoons nutmeg

1½ teaspoons cinnamon

1½ teaspoons ginger

½ cup sprinkles, divided

In large bowl, combine chocolate chips, milk, nutmeg, cinnamon, and ginger. Mix well. Stir in half of sprinkles. Pour into buttered 9x9-inch baking dish. Spread out and top with remaining sprinkles. Chill. Cut into squares.

YIELD: 30 PIECES

Triple Threats

1 (12 ounce) package milk chocolate chips

2 tablespoons shortening

30 caramels

3 tablespoons butter

2 tablespoons water

1 cup unsalted dry roasted peanuts, coarsely chopped

In top of double boiler, combine chocolate chips and shortening. Bring water to boil. Reduce heat to low and cook until melted, stirring occasionally. Spread half of chocolate mixture evenly in foil-lined 8x8-inch pan. Chill for 15 minutes. Remove remaining chocolate mixture from double boiler and keep warm. In top of double boiler, combine caramels, butter, and water. Bring water in bottom of double boiler to boil. Reduce heat to low and cook, stirring occasionally, until smooth. Spread caramel mixture over chocolate mixture in pan. Chill for 15 minutes. Spread remaining chocolate over caramel mixture. Chill for 1 hour. Cut into squares.

YIELD: 1¾ POUNDS

Rum and Cinnamon Pecans

2 egg whites

3 cups pecans

1 cup sugar

1 teaspoon cinnamon

1 teaspoon rum flavoring

½ teaspoon vanilla

2 tablespoons water

Preheat oven to 300 degrees. In large bowl, whisk egg whites until frothy. Add pecans and stir until coated. In small bowl, combine sugar, cinnamon, rum flavoring, vanilla, and water. Pour sugar mixture over nuts. Spread in single layer on parchment-lined baking sheet. Bake for 25 minutes, stirring every 10 minutes. Cool completely and store in airtight container.

YIELD: 3 CUPS

My Favorite Christmas Candy Recipes

Recipe:

INGREDIENTS:

DIRECTIONS:

YIELD:

Recipe:

INGREDIENTS:

DIRECTIONS:

YIELD:

Recipe:

Ingredients:

Directions:

Yield:

Recipe:

Ingredients:

Directions:

Yield:

Recipe:

Ingredients:

Directions:

Yield:

On the sixth day of Christmas my true love sent to me:

Six Cookies a-Cooling

For centuries men have kept an appointment with Christmas. Christmas means fellowship, feasting, giving and receiving, a time of good cheer, home.

W. J. RONALD TUCKER

Father God, thank You for family and home, safe places and loving faces. Thank You for the gift of fellowship. We are happy to be Your people. Amen.

Mary said, My soul doth magnify the Lord,
and my spirit hath rejoiced in God my Saviour.

LUKE 1:46–47 KJV

Snickerdoodles *

½ cup butter

½ cup shortening

2 eggs

2½ cups flour

2 teaspoons cream of tartar

1 teaspoon baking soda

½ teaspoon salt

2 tablespoons sugar

2 teaspoons cinnamon

Preheat oven to 350 degrees. In large bowl, cream together butter, shortening, and eggs. Add flour, cream of tartar, baking soda, and salt. In small bowl, combine sugar and cinnamon. Roll walnut-size balls of dough in sugar mixture and place on ungreased cookie sheet. Bake for 8 to 10 minutes.

YIELD: 3 DOZEN

Orange Slice Cookies

1 cup butter, softened

1 cup packed brown sugar

1 cup sugar

2 eggs

1 teaspoon vanilla

2 cups flour

1 teaspoon baking soda

½ teaspoon salt

1 cup quick-cooking oats

1 cup sweetened flaked coconut

1 cup pecans

1 cup orange candy slices, chopped and dusted with flour

Preheat oven to 350 degrees. In large bowl, cream butter with sugars. Add eggs and vanilla. Mix well. Add flour, baking soda, salt, and oats. Mix well. Stir in coconut, pecans, and candy pieces. Drop by spoonful on greased cookie sheet. Bake for 10 minutes. Cool completely and store in airtight container.

YIELD: 4 DOZEN

Butter Yums *

2 cups salted butter, softened

2 cups powdered sugar

4 cups flour

1 teaspoon vanilla

Preheat oven to 350 degrees. In large bowl, cream butter and powdered sugar. Add flour and vanilla. Roll into walnut-size balls. Place on ungreased cookie sheet, flattening with floured bottom of drinking glass. Bake for 15 minutes or until slightly brown. Cool on rack.

YIELD: 6 DOZEN

Candy Canes

1 cup butter, softened

2 teaspoons vanilla

2½ cups flour

½ teaspoon salt

1½ cups quick-cooking oats

1 cup powdered sugar, divided

2 tablespoons water

1 tablespoon heavy cream

Red food coloring

Preheat oven to 325 degrees. In large bowl, cream butter and vanilla. In medium bowl, combine flour, salt, oats, and ½ cup powdered sugar. Add to creamed mixture. Add enough water to cause dough to stick together. Chill for 1 hour. Break off 1 spoonful of dough. Roll and twist to form cane and place on greased cookie sheet. Repeat with each spoonful. Bake for 25 minutes. While cookies bake, combine remaining ½ cup powdered sugar with cream and stir to create thin icing. Divide into 2 small bowls. Add red coloring to one. When cookies have cooled, ice with white icing and then stripe with red icing.

YIELD: 4 DOZEN

Angel Bites *

1 cup finely chopped walnuts

½ cup cocoa

1 cup sugar

3 tablespoons vegetable oil

8 egg whites

½ teaspoon salt

¼ cup powdered sugar

Preheat oven to 350 degrees. In large bowl, combine walnuts, cocoa, sugar, and oil. Set aside. In medium bowl, beat egg whites and salt until stiff peaks form. Fold ⅓ of beaten egg whites into nut mixture. Add remaining egg whites. Blend carefully. Spoon into greased or nonstick mini-muffin pans. Bake for 12 minutes. Cool for 5 minutes. Remove from pan and sprinkle with powdered sugar.

YIELD: 4 DOZEN

Almond Crispies

½ cup butter, softened

⅓ cup shortening

1 cup packed brown sugar

1 teaspoon almond extract

½ teaspoon salt

2 cups flour

¾ cup finely chopped almonds

Preheat oven to 350 degrees. In large bowl, combine butter, shortening, brown sugar, and almond extract. Cream well. Add salt, flour, and almonds. Mix well. Roll out dough on floured board to ½-inch thickness. Cut into Christmas shapes. Place on ungreased cookie sheet and bake for 8 to 10 minutes or until light golden brown.

YIELD: 4½ DOZEN

Honey Pecan Balls

1 cup butter, softened

½ cup sugar

1 teaspoon vanilla

1 teaspoon almond extract

2 cups flour

1 cup finely chopped pecans

1 cup sweetened flaked coconut, chopped

½ cup honey

⅓ cup pineapple juice

2 teaspoons vinegar

2 tablespoons butter

Preheat oven to 350 degrees. In large bowl, cream butter, sugar, vanilla, and almond extract. Add flour, pecans, and coconut. Mix thoroughly. Roll dough into 1-inch balls. Place on ungreased baking sheet and bake for 18 minutes or until light golden brown. In saucepan, combine honey, pineapple juice, vinegar, and butter. Simmer for 5 minutes. Brush cookies with honey mixture. After 3 minutes, flip cookies and brush backs generously with honey mixture. When completely cool, store in airtight container.

YIELD: 6 DOZEN

Sugar and Spice Cookies

3 cups flour

1 teaspoon baking soda

1 teaspoon cream of tartar

½ teaspoon salt

½ cup butter, softened

½ cup shortening

2 cups packed brown sugar

2 eggs

1 teaspoon vanilla

1 cup quick-cooking oats

½ cup sugar

4 teaspoons cinnamon

Preheat oven to 350 degrees. In medium bowl, sift together flour, baking soda, cream of tartar, and salt. In large bowl, cream butter, shortening, and brown sugar. Add eggs and vanilla. Mix well. Stir in flour mixture. Add oats. Mix thoroughly. Chill for 1 hour. Divide dough into 3 parts. On floured board, shape into rolls 12 inches long. Chill for 6 hours. Cut into ¼-inch slices. Mix sugar and cinnamon in small bowl. Dip both sides of each slice in sugar mixture. Bake for 10 minutes or until golden brown.

YIELD: 9 DOZEN

Cashew Delights

2¼ cups flour

½ teaspoon baking soda

½ teaspoon cream of tartar

1 cup butter, softened

¾ cup packed brown sugar

½ cup sugar

1 egg

1 teaspoon vanilla

1½ cups finely chopped cashews

Preheat oven to 350 degrees. In medium bowl, sift together flour, baking soda, and cream of tartar. Set aside. In large bowl, cream butter, brown sugar, and sugar. Blend in egg and vanilla. Add flour mixture. Combine thoroughly without overstirring. Add cashews. Drop by spoonful onto greased baking sheet. Bake for 12 to 15 minutes or until golden brown.

YIELD: 5 DOZEN

Christmas Morning Wake-Ups

½ cup butter, softened

2 teaspoons instant coffee granules

½ cup instant hot cocoa mix

½ cup powdered sugar

1 tablespoon light cream

1½ cups flour

½ cup chopped pecans

Preheat oven to 350 degrees. In large bowl, cream butter, coffee granules, cocoa mix, powdered sugar, and cream. Mix well. Add flour. Mix thoroughly. Chill dough. Roll out on floured surface to 14x10-inch rectangle. Sprinkle with pecans. Press into dough. Cut into 2-inch squares. Place squares on ungreased cookie sheet. Bake for 9 to 12 minutes or until golden brown.

YIELD: 3 DOZEN

Chocolate Cherry Chews

1 cup flour

⅓ cup packed brown sugar

½ cup butter

36 maraschino cherries

6 ounces semisweet chocolate squares

Preheat oven to 350 degrees. In medium bowl, combine flour and brown sugar. Mix well. Cut in butter with pastry cutter until mixture resembles coarse crumbles. Press into ungreased 8x8-inch baking pan. Bake for 18 minutes or until golden brown. While warm, cut into 36 squares. Place squares on waxed paper. Place 1 well-drained cherry on top of each square. Melt chocolate in top of double boiler until smooth. Top each cherry with 1 teaspoon chocolate. Let stand until chocolate hardens. Store in flat container. Do not stack.

YIELD: 36 SQUARES

Raisin and Spice Oatmeal Cookies

1 cup flour

1 teaspoon baking powder

1 teaspoon cinnamon

¼ teaspoon nutmeg

½ teaspoon salt

¾ cup shortening

1 cup packed brown sugar

2 eggs

⅓ cup milk, divided

3 cups quick-cooking oats

1 cup raisins

Preheat oven to 375 degrees. In large bowl, combine flour, baking powder, cinnamon, nutmeg, and salt. Mix well. Add shortening, brown sugar, eggs, and half of milk. Beat for 2 minutes or until smooth. Stir in remaining milk and oats. Mix well. Add raisins. Stir well. Drop by spoonful onto greased baking sheet and bake for 12 to 15 minutes.

YIELD: 4 DOZEN

Holiday Peanut Butter Bars

1¼ cups packed brown sugar

½ cup butter, softened

½ cup shortening

¼ cup crunchy peanut butter

¼ teaspoon salt

1 egg yolk, beaten

1 teaspoon vanilla

3 cups flour

6 ounces semisweet chocolate chips

½ cup crunchy peanut butter

1½ cups rice cereal

Preheat oven to 350 degrees. In large bowl, cream brown sugar, butter, shortening, and ¼ cup peanut butter. Add salt, egg yolk, and vanilla. Mix well. Add flour. Mix well. Press firmly into ungreased 15x10-inch jelly roll pan. Bake for 28 minutes. Cool slightly. Melt chocolate chips in top of double boiler. Stir in ½ cup peanut butter and rice cereal. Spread over baked cookie dough. Let stand until chocolate hardens. Cut into squares.

YIELD: 3½ DOZEN

Iced Jubilee Cookies

½ cup shortening

½ cup sugar

1 cup packed brown sugar

2 eggs

1 cup evaporated milk

1 teaspoon vanilla

2¾ cups flour

½ teaspoon baking soda

1 teaspoon salt

1 cup chopped pecans

2 tablespoons butter

2 cups powdered sugar

¼ cup evaporated milk

Preheat oven to 375 degrees. In large bowl, combine shortening, sugar, brown sugar, and eggs. Mix well. Add evaporated milk and vanilla. Stir in flour, baking soda, and salt. Fold in pecans. Chill. Drop by spoonful 2 inches apart on greased cookie sheet. Bake for 10 minutes or until lightly browned. In saucepan, cook butter until lightly browned. Add powdered sugar and milk. Cook until golden brown. Spread over cooled cookies.

YIELD: 3 DOZEN

Candied Fruit Jumbles

1 cup candied red and green cherries

1¼ cups flour, divided

1 cup coarsely chopped pecans

1 cup chopped dates

¼ cup milk

1 teaspoon cider vinegar

½ cup butter, softened

¾ cup packed brown sugar

1 egg

2 teaspoons grated lemon rind

½ teaspoon salt

½ teaspoon baking soda

Preheat oven to 375 degrees. Mix candied cherries with ¼ cup flour. Combine candied cherries, pecans, dates, milk, and vinegar. Let stand for 10 minutes. In large bowl, cream together butter, brown sugar, egg, lemon rind, remaining 1 cup flour, salt, and baking soda. Fold in fruit and nut mixture. Drop by spoonful onto cookie sheet and bake for 12 minutes. Cool.

YIELD: 3 DOZEN

Christmas Lights

1 cup butter, softened

1½ cups sugar

3 eggs

1 teaspoon vanilla

4 cups cake flour

1 teaspoon salt

1 teaspoon baking powder

½ cup chopped candied cherries

½ cup chopped candied pineapple

½ cup chopped pecans

Preheat oven to 375 degrees. In large bowl, cream butter, sugar, eggs, and vanilla. Add flour, salt, and baking powder. Blend well. Stir in fruit and pecans. Divide dough in half. Form each half into long roll and wrap in waxed paper. Chill for 1 hour. Slice cookies. Place on cookie sheet and bake for 8 minutes.

YIELD: 5 DOZEN

Rich Walnut Cookies

4 eggs

2 cups packed brown sugar

½ cup flour

½ teaspoon baking powder

½ teaspoon salt

1 pound chopped walnuts

Preheat oven to 375 degrees. In large bowl, beat eggs well. Gradually add brown sugar to eggs until well mixed. In medium bowl, sift together flour, baking powder, and salt. Add to egg mixture. Combine well. Stir in walnuts. Drop by spoonful onto greased cookie sheet and bake for 12 minutes.

YIELD: 4 DOZEN

Mrs. Claus's Christmas Giveaways

1 cup butter, softened

⅔ cup powdered sugar, sifted

1 teaspoon vanilla

½ teaspoon almond extract

2 cups flour

¼ teaspoon salt

6 ounces semisweet chocolate chips

3 tablespoons powdered sugar

2 tablespoons red and green sprinkles

Preheat oven to 350 degrees. In large bowl, cream butter and ⅔ cup powdered sugar. Add vanilla and almond extract. Stir well. Add flour and salt. Mix thoroughly. Chill dough. On floured board, roll out half of dough into large rectangle. Cut in half. Cut into 2x1-inch strips. Place on ungreased cookie sheet and bake for 12 to 15 minutes. While cookies are cooling, melt chocolate in top of double boiler. Add powdered sugar and stir until smooth. Dip one end of each cookie in chocolate and place on waxed paper. Before chocolate has time to set, add red and green sprinkles.

YIELD: 4 DOZEN

Dancer's Rock Cookies

1 cup butter, softened

1½ cups sugar

3 eggs, beaten

3 cups flour (set aside ⅛ cup)

1 tablespoon cocoa

1 teaspoon nutmeg

1 teaspoon mace

1 teaspoon cinnamon

½ teaspoon ginger

½ teaspoon allspice

¾ teaspoon baking soda

1 tablespoon strong coffee

⅓ cup chopped candied cherries

⅓ cup chopped candied pineapple

½ cup chopped dates

¼ cup chopped candied orange peel

½ cup currants

1 cup raisins

2 cups chopped mixed nuts

Preheat oven to 325 degrees. In large bowl, cream butter with sugar until fluffy. Add eggs and beat well. Add flour, cocoa, spices, and baking soda. Mix well. Add coffee. Mix well. In separate bowl, combine cherries, pineapple, dates, and orange peel. Dredge in reserved ⅛ cup flour. Add to flour mixture. Mix well. Add currants, raisins, and nuts. Mix well. Drop by spoonful on greased cookie sheet. Bake for 12 to 15 minutes or until tan (not brown).

Yield: 6 dozen

Chocolate Molasses Cookies

¾ cup butter, softened

1 cup sugar

1 egg

¼ cup molasses

2 cups flour

2 teaspoons baking soda

¼ teaspoon salt

1 teaspoon cinnamon

¾ teaspoon ginger

½ teaspoon cloves

1¼ cups semisweet chocolate chips

Preheat oven to 350 degrees. In large bowl, cream butter with sugar. Add egg and molasses and beat well at medium speed with electric mixer. In medium bowl, combine flour, baking soda, salt, cinnamon, ginger, and cloves. Add to creamed mixture. Stir well. Add chocolate chips. Mix well. Drop by spoonful onto greased cookie sheets. Bake for 8 to 10 minutes. Transfer to rack and cool completely.

YIELD: 4½ DOZEN

My Favorite Christmas Cookie Recipes

Recipe:

INGREDIENTS:

DIRECTIONS:

YIELD:

Recipe:

INGREDIENTS:

DIRECTIONS:

YIELD:

Recipe:..

INGREDIENTS:...
....
....

DIRECTIONS:...
....
....
....
....

YIELD:...

Recipe:..

INGREDIENTS:...
....
....

DIRECTIONS:...
....
....
....
....

YIELD:...

Recipe:..

INGREDIENTS:...
....
....

DIRECTIONS:...
....
....
....
....

YIELD:...

On the seventh day of Christmas my true love sent to me:

Seven Desserts a-Delighting

Blessed is the season which engages
the whole world in a conspiracy of love!

HAMILTON WRIGHT MABIE

Jesus, You are the sweetness of life. Your grace warms our hearts, and Your love makes us rejoice. Thank You for Your constant presence in our lives. Amen.

I will be fully satisfied as with the richest of foods;
with singing lips my mouth will praise you.

Psalm 63:5 niv

Pumpkin Roll *

1 cup sugar

3 whole eggs

¾ cup flour

⅔ cup canned pumpkin

2 teaspoons cinnamon

1 teaspoon baking soda

½ teaspoon salt

½ cup powdered sugar

Powdered sugar, for tea towel

8 ounces cream cheese, softened

¼ cup butter, softened

1 cup powdered sugar

1 teaspoon vanilla

¼ teaspoon salt

Preheat oven to 375 degrees. Cream together sugar and eggs. Add flour, pumpkin, cinnamon, baking soda, ½ teaspoon salt, and ½ cup powdered sugar and mix well. Lightly spray jelly roll pan and line with waxed paper. Pour in batter and bake for 15 minutes. Cool in pan for 5 minutes. Flip out onto tea towel sprinkled with powdered sugar. Peel off waxed paper. Gently roll up cake and let stand for 30 minutes. For filling, cream together cream cheese, butter, and 1 cup powdered sugar. Add vanilla and ¼ teaspoon salt. Blend well. Unroll cake and spread with filling. Gently roll up again and refrigerate for 2 hours. Slice into pinwheel servings.

YIELD: 10 TO 12 SERVINGS

Gumdrop Fruitcake

1 cup butter

1 cup sugar

1½ cups applesauce

1 egg, well beaten

1 teaspoon cinnamon

½ teaspoon baking soda

½ cup hot water

4 cups flour

1 (14 ounce) package gumdrops

1 (1 pound) box raisins

1½ cups chopped pecans

2 cups chopped dates

Preheat oven to 225 degrees. In large bowl, cream together butter and sugar. Add applesauce, egg, and cinnamon. Dissolve baking soda in hot water. Add to creamed mixture. Add flour and mix well. Add gumdrops, raisins, pecans, and dates. Mix well. Grease and flour 2 angel food cake pans. Pour batter into pans. Bake for 3 hours.

YIELD: 2 LARGE FRUITCAKES

Scalloped Apples *

6 Granny Smith apples, peeled, cored, and sliced

1 teaspoon lemon juice

¾ cup brown sugar

4 tablespoons butter

2 eggs, beaten

½ teaspoon cinnamon

½ teaspoon nutmeg

½ teaspoon salt

2 cups crushed buttery crackers

Preheat oven to 350 degrees. In large saucepan, cook apples for about 15 minutes, until slightly softened. Stir in lemon juice, brown sugar, butter, eggs, cinnamon, nutmeg, and salt. Grease 11x9-inch baking dish and cover bottom with layer of cracker crumbs, followed by layer of apple mixture. Keep alternating remaining ingredients. Reserve some crumbs for top. Bake for 45 minutes.

YIELD: 6 SERVINGS

Cherry Cream Cheese Tarts

1 (12 ounce) box vanilla wafers

3 (8 ounce) packages cream cheese, softened

1 cup sugar

4 eggs, beaten

1 (21 ounce) can cherry pie filling

Preheat oven to 350 degrees. Place liners in 36 muffin cups. Place 1 vanilla wafer flat-side up in each cup. In medium mixing bowl, combine cream cheese, sugar, and eggs with electric mixer until light and fluffy. Spoon batter over wafers, filling ⅔ full. Bake for 25 minutes. Spoon pie filling on tarts.

YIELD: 36 TARTS

Eggnog Chiffon Pie *

꧁ ⁘꧂

1½ cups sugar cookie crumbs

6 tablespoons butter

2 envelopes unflavored gelatin

⅓ cup water

2½ cups eggnog

1 cup heavy cream, whipped

1 teaspoon nutmeg

2 tablespoons cookie crumbs, for garnish

8 maraschino cherries

In small bowl, mix cookie crumbs and butter until well blended. Press firmly onto bottom and sides of ungreased 9-inch pie pan. Chill. In small saucepan, soften gelatin in water and stir over low heat until well dissolved. In bowl, mix gelatin and eggnog. Chill just until syrupy. Fold in whipped cream and spoon into crust. Sprinkle lightly with nutmeg. Chill until firm. Sprinkle additional cookie crumbs on top. Add cherries.

YIELD: 8 SERVINGS

Cranberry Crisp

꧁ ⁘꧂

1 (16 ounce) can whole cranberry sauce

½ cup quick-cooking oats

¼ cup flour

½ cup packed brown sugar

¼ cup butter

Preheat oven to 350 degrees. Spread cranberry sauce in bottom of 9-inch pie pan. In medium bowl, combine oats, flour, and brown sugar. Cut in butter until crumbly. Sprinkle over cranberries. Bake for 25 minutes.

YIELD: 6 SERVINGS

Chocolate Upside-Down Cake

1 cup flour	1 teaspoon vanilla
½ tablespoon cocoa	2 tablespoons butter, melted
½ teaspoon salt	½ cup chopped nuts
¾ cup sugar	1¼ cups sugar
2 tablespoons baking powder	4 tablespoons cocoa
¾ cup milk	1½ cups hot water

Preheat oven to 350 degrees. In large bowl, sift together flour, ½ tablespoon cocoa, salt, ¾ cup sugar, and baking powder. Mix until smooth. Add milk, vanilla, butter, and nuts. Pour into 9- or 10-inch cast-iron skillet. Combine 1¼ cups sugar and 4 tablespoons cocoa. Sprinkle over batter. Carefully pour hot water over batter and sugar mixture. Bake for 45 minutes. While cake is hot from oven, invert on large cake plate.

YIELD: 12 SERVINGS

Mahogany Cake with Mocha Filling

½ cup butter, softened

2 cups sugar

3 eggs, well beaten

⅞ cup strong black coffee, divided

2 cups flour, divided

4 teaspoons baking powder

1½ squares bittersweet chocolate, melted

1 tablespoon vinegar

1 cup coarsely chopped walnuts

¼ teaspoon salt

⅓ teaspoon baking soda

3 tablespoons hot water

1 cup butter

3½ cups powdered sugar

6 tablespoons cocoa

5 tablespoons black coffee, divided

1 teaspoon vanilla

Preheat oven to 375 degrees. In large bowl, cream butter and sugar until fluffy. Add eggs and half of coffee. Beat well. Add 1 cup flour, baking powder, chocolate, vinegar, walnuts, and salt. Dissolve baking soda in hot water and add to mixture. Beat until smooth. Add remaining coffee and flour alternately. Beat well. Pour into 2 greased and floured 9-inch cake pans. Bake for 25 minutes. In large bowl, cream butter. Combine powdered sugar and cocoa. Cream enough sugar mixture into butter until it becomes stiff. Add 2 tablespoons coffee. Continue adding sugar mixture and coffee alternately until proper consistency. Add vanilla. Spread between layers and use to ice cake.

Yield: 15 servings

Cranberry Pudding Pie

1¼ cups whole cranberries

¼ cup packed brown sugar

¼ cup chopped walnuts

1 egg

½ cup sugar

½ cup flour

⅓ cup butter, melted

Preheat oven to 325 degrees. Spread cranberries in greased 9-inch pie pan. Sprinkle with brown sugar and walnuts. Beat egg until thick. Gradually add sugar, beating until blended well. Add flour and butter. Beat well. Pour batter over cranberries. Bake for 45 minutes.

YIELD: 6 SERVINGS

Holiday Fruit Pudding

2 cups flour

¾ teaspoon baking soda

½ teaspoon salt

½ teaspoon cinnamon

¼ teaspoon nutmeg

⅔ cup sugar

½ cup shortening, creamed well

1 egg

1 tablespoon milk

1½ cups pared, coarsely shredded apples

½ cup chopped dates

½ cup raisins

Preheat oven to 350 degrees. In medium bowl, sift together flour, baking soda, salt, cinnamon, and nutmeg. Set aside. In large bowl, cream sugar into shortening. Add egg and milk. Beat well. Add flour mixture gradually, mixing thoroughly. Stir in apples, dates, and raisins. Pour into 8x8-inch baking dish, greased on bottom only. Bake for 45 minutes.

YIELD: 8 TO 10 SERVINGS

Christmas in the Islands Pie

4 cups (4 medium) apples, pared and sliced

1 cup crushed pineapple

⅔ cup sugar

1 teaspoon cinnamon

3 tablespoons flour

2 (9 inch) piecrusts

1 tablespoon butter, melted

Preheat oven to 425 degrees. In large bowl, combine apples, pineapple, sugar, cinnamon, and flour. Mix well. Place crust in 9-inch pie pan. Add filling. Cover with remaining crust. Crimp edges. Cut slit in top crust for steam. Brush with butter. Bake for 10 minutes. Reduce heat to 350 degrees. Continue baking for 25 minutes or until apples are tender.

YIELD: 8 SERVINGS

Candy Apples

8 medium red apples

8 flat wooden skewers

2 cups sugar

1 cup light corn syrup

½ cup water

¼ cup red cinnamon candies

10 drops red food coloring

Wash and dry apples. Inset skewers into stem holes. In heavy 2-quart saucepan, combine sugar, corn syrup, and water. Cook over medium heat, stirring constantly, until mixture boils or reaches hard-ball stage (250 degrees). Add candies and continue to cook until temperature reaches soft-crack stage (285 degrees). Remove from heat and stir in food coloring. Holding each apple by its skewer, twirl in syrup until whole apple is covered. Allow excess to drip off. Then twirl apple in syrup again. Place on greased cookie sheet to cool.

YIELD: 8 APPLES

Maple Custard Pie

1 (9 inch) piecrust

2 tablespoons flour

½ cup maple syrup

¼ cup water

¼ teaspoon maple flavoring

1 egg yolk, slightly beaten

1 tablespoon butter

2 eggs, slightly beaten

¼ cup sugar

¼ teaspoon salt

1 cup hot scalded milk

1 cup hot scalded cream

Preheat oven to 425 degrees. Place crust in bottom of 9-inch pie pan. Bake for 2 minutes. Remove from oven. In medium saucepan, combine flour, maple syrup, water, and maple flavoring. Mix until smooth. Add egg yolk and butter. Cook over medium heat, stirring constantly, until thickened. Pour immediately into partially baked crust. In bowl, combine eggs, sugar, salt, milk, and cream. Pour custard mixture against inside of large spoon over maple mixture. Bake for 10 minutes. Reduce heat to 350 degrees. Continue baking for 10 to 15 minutes.

YIELD: 8 SERVINGS

Lime Chiffon Pie

1 envelope unflavored gelatin

¼ cup cold water

3 eggs, separated

¾ cup light corn syrup

1 teaspoon grated lime rind

½ cup lime juice

¼ cup sugar

1 (9 inch) graham cracker crust, baked

In heavy 2-quart saucepan, stir gelatin into water. Add egg yolks, corn syrup, lime rind, and lime juice. Cook over low heat, stirring constantly, until slightly thickened (do not boil). Cool. In separate bowl, beat egg whites on high speed with electric mixer until soft peaks form. Gradually beat in sugar until stiff peaks form. Fold into yolk mixture. Spoon into crust and chill until firm.

Yield: 8 servings

Cranberry Walnut Pie

1 (9 inch) piecrust

3 eggs

1 cup light corn syrup

⅔ cup sugar

2 tablespoons butter, melted

⅛ teaspoon salt

1 cup chopped cranberries

¾ cup coarsely chopped walnuts

1 tablespoon grated orange rind

Preheat oven to 350 degrees. Place piecrust in 9-inch pie pan. In large bowl, beat eggs slightly. Stir in corn syrup, sugar, butter, and salt. Blend well. Stir in cranberries, walnuts, and orange rind. Pour into crust. Bake for 1 hour.

YIELD: 8 SERVINGS

No-Bake Holiday Cake

3 cups graham cracker crumbs

1 tablespoon grated lemon rind

½ teaspoon cinnamon

⅛ teaspoon allspice

⅛ teaspoon ginger

1 pound mixed candied fruit, chopped

1 (3.5 ounce) can sweetened flaked coconut

1 cup chopped pecans

1 cup golden raisins

½ cup light corn syrup

1 teaspoon rum flavoring

2 tablespoons lemon juice

In large bowl, stir together graham cracker crumbs, lemon rind, cinnamon, allspice, and ginger. Stir in candied fruit, coconut, pecans, and raisins until well blended. In small bowl, combine corn syrup, rum flavoring, and lemon juice. Add to crumb mixture and mix well. Press firmly into foil-lined standard loaf pan. Cover tightly with foil and refrigerate for 4 days. Remove from pan. Remove foil. Cut into thin slices.

YIELD: 1 (3 POUND) LOAF

Snowbird Bars

¾ cup flour

1 cup sugar

1 teaspoon baking powder

¼ teaspoon salt

2 cups chopped dates

1 cup walnuts

3 eggs, beaten

1 teaspoon vanilla

2 tablespoons milk

1 cup powdered sugar

Preheat oven to 325 degrees. In large bowl, sift together flour, sugar, baking powder, and salt. Add dates, walnuts, eggs, vanilla, and milk. Mix well. Spread in greased 8x8-inch pan. Bake for 40 minutes. Cool completely. Cut into squares. Then cut each square in half and roll in powdered sugar.

YIELD: 18 BARS

Orange Marmalade Bread Pudding

5 slices day-old bread with crust, toasted

3 tablespoons butter, softened

¾ cup orange marmalade

3 eggs, slightly beaten

1¾ cups milk

3 teaspoons lemon juice

⅛ teaspoon nutmeg

½ cup heavy cream

Preheat oven to 300 degrees. Spread toast slices with butter and marmalade. Cut into cubes and place in buttered casserole dish. In small bowl, mix eggs with milk, lemon juice, and nutmeg. Pour over toast cubes. Bake for 45 minutes. Serve warm with cream.

YIELD: 5 SERVINGS

Big Bad Butter Cake

2 cups flour

2½ teaspoons baking powder

1 teaspoon salt

1¾ cups sugar

⅓ cup nonfat dry milk

1 cup plus 2 tablespoons butter, melted

4 eggs, divided

2½ teaspoons vanilla, divided

1 (8 ounce) package cream cheese, softened

3½ cups powdered sugar

Preheat oven to 350 degrees. In large bowl, combine flour, baking powder, salt, sugar, and dry milk. Stir well. Add butter, 2 eggs, and 1½ teaspoons vanilla. With electric mixer on medium speed, beat until well blended. Pour into greased 15x10-inch jelly roll pan. In separate bowl, beat cream cheese with electric mixer on medium speed. Add remaining 2 eggs and 1 teaspoon vanilla. Beat well. Add powdered sugar and beat until mixture is smooth. Spread over batter in pan. Bake for 25 to 30 minutes. Cool in pan and cut into squares.

YIELD: 40 SERVINGS

Dutch Cherry Cake

2 cups flour

2¼ teaspoons baking powder

½ teaspoon salt

1 cup sugar, divided

2 eggs, separated

½ cup milk

⅓ cup butter, melted

2½ cups canned unsweetened red cherries, drained (juice reserved) and divided

3 tablespoons brown sugar

1 teaspoon cinnamon

1 tablespoon cornstarch

3 tablespoons sugar

Boiling water

⅛ teaspoon salt

1 tablespoon butter

⅛ teaspoon almond extract

Preheat oven to 400 degrees. In large bowl, sift together flour, baking powder, salt, and ¾ cup sugar. In separate bowl, beat egg yolks. Add milk and butter. Stir and incorporate into flour mixture until smooth. Beat egg whites until stiff, adding remaining ¼ cup sugar. Fold into batter along with 1 cup cherries. Pour into buttered 11x7-inch baking pan. Sprinkle batter with brown sugar and cinnamon. Bake for 35 minutes. In saucepan, heat cherry juice to boiling. In small bowl, blend cornstarch, sugar, and 3 tablespoons boiling water to make smooth paste. Add to hot juice and stir over heat until sauce boils and thickens. Stir in salt, butter, almond extract, and remaining 1½ cups cherries. Pour over warm cake.

YIELD: 6 TO 8 SERVINGS

My Favorite Christmas Dessert Recipes

Recipe: ....
INGREDIENTS: ....
....
....
....
DIRECTIONS: ....
....
....
....
....
....
YIELD: ....

Recipe: ....
INGREDIENTS: ....
....
....
....
DIRECTIONS: ....
....
....
....
....
YIELD: ....

Recipe:..

INGREDIENTS: ....

....

....

DIRECTIONS: ....

....

....

....

....

YIELD: ....

Recipe:..

INGREDIENTS: ....

....

....

DIRECTIONS: ....

....

....

....

....

YIELD: ....

Recipe:..

INGREDIENTS: ....

....

....

DIRECTIONS: ....

....

....

....

....

YIELD: ....

On the eighth day of Christmas my true love sent to me:

Eight Kids a-Cooking

Gifts of time and love are surely the basic ingredients of a truly merry Christmas.

Peg Bracken

The wise men brought their gifts for the newborn King, the human representation of You, our Father God. Thank You for coming to us when we could not come to You. Thank You for the gift of Your Son. Amen.

The Word became flesh and made his dwelling among us. We have seen his glory, the glory of the one and only Son, who came from the Father, full of grace and truth.

JOHN 1:14 NIV

No-Bake Krispy Krunch Bars *

2 cups peanut butter

2 cups buttercream frosting

2½ cups rice cereal

4 tablespoons soft butter

½ cup peanuts

1 cup semisweet chocolate chips

1 tablespoon butter

Mix together peanut butter, frosting, rice cereal, 4 tablespoons butter, and peanuts. Press into 13x9-inch pan. In saucepan, melt chocolate chips and 1 tablespoon butter. Drizzle over crunch mixture. Chill for 1 hour.

YIELD: 24 BARS

Creamy Christmas Fudge

4 cups sugar

1 (14.5 ounce) can evaporated milk

½ cup butter

⅛ teaspoon salt

2 (6 ounce) packages semisweet chocolate chips

16 ounces marshmallow crème

1 cup pecan pieces

1 teaspoon vanilla

In heavy 2-quart saucepan, combine sugar, milk, butter, and salt. Cook over medium heat, stirring constantly, until mixture comes to boil. Continue cooking, stirring occasionally, until mixture reaches soft-ball stage (235 degrees). Butter sides and bottom of 11x9-inch baking pan. Remove fudge mixture from heat. Add chocolate chips, marshmallow crème, pecans, and vanilla. Stir until chocolate melts and is well blended. Pour into pan. Cool completely. Cut into squares.

YIELD: 50 SQUARES

Green Eggs and Ham *

½ pound ham steak

1 tablespoon butter

4 eggs

1 drop green food coloring

½ teaspoon salt

½ teaspoon pepper

Slice ham into serving-size pieces and brown in butter. Scramble eggs and stir in food coloring, salt, and pepper. Serve on top of ham.

YIELD: 4 SERVINGS

Roly-Polies

2¾ cups flour

2 teaspoons cream of tartar

1 teaspoon baking soda

⅛ teaspoon salt

1 cup shortening

1½ cups sugar

2 eggs

2 tablespoons sugar

2 teaspoons cinnamon

In medium bowl, sift together flour, cream of tartar, baking soda, and salt. In large bowl, cream shortening with sugar. Add eggs and beat well. Add flour mixture and stir until completely moistened. Chill dough for 2 hours. Preheat oven to 350 degrees. In small bowl, combine sugar and cinnamon. Shape dough into small balls and roll in sugar-cinnamon mixture. Place on greased cookie sheet. Bake for 10 to 12 minutes.

YIELD: 6 DOZEN

Brownie Toast

¼ cup brown sugar

4 teaspoons sweetened flaked coconut

4 slices bread

2 tablespoons butter

Line broiler pan with aluminum foil. In small bowl, mix together brown sugar and coconut. Place bread slices on foil. Turn on broiler and toast bread until lightly browned. Remove from oven. Turn slices over. Butter untoasted sides generously. Top each slice with 1 tablespoon sugar mixture. Toast until bubbly and brown.

YIELD: 4 SERVINGS

Tootsie's Tuna Casserole

1 (10.5 ounce) can cream of mushroom soup

½ teaspoon salt

½ cup milk

1 (7 ounce) can tuna

¾ cup crushed potato chips

Preheat oven to 350 degrees. In small bowl, mix soup, salt, and milk. Drain tuna and scatter evenly in bottom of greased 1½-quart casserole dish. Pour soup mixture over tuna. Sprinkle with potato chips. Bake for 25 minutes.

YIELD: 4 SERVINGS

Elfish Eggs

6 eggs

½ teaspoon salt

⅛ teaspoon pepper

1 teaspoon mustard

1 teaspoon cider vinegar

3 tablespoons mayonnaise

1 tablespoon paprika

Place eggs in small saucepan. Add cold water to ½ inch above top of eggs. Bring to boil. Reduce heat to medium and boil for 20 minutes. Remove from heat and place in cold water until cool enough to handle. Peel eggs under running water. Cut each egg in half lengthwise. Remove yolks carefully. Place whites on serving plate. In small bowl, mash yolks. Add salt, pepper, mustard, vinegar, and mayonnaise. Combine well. Fill each egg white with yolk mixture. Return to plate. Sprinkle with paprika. Cover and keep in refrigerator until ready to serve.

YIELD: 12 SERVINGS

Popcorn Balls

6 quarts popped corn	½ cup dark corn syrup
¾ cup brown sugar	2 tablespoons cider vinegar
¾ cup sugar	¼ cup butter
½ cup water	½ teaspoon baking soda

Place popcorn in large pan. In heavy 2-quart saucepan, combine sugars, water, corn syrup, and vinegar. Cook until mixture reaches thread stage (230 degrees). Add butter. Continue to cook to hard-ball stage (260 degrees). Add baking soda and remove from heat. Pour over popcorn. As soon as you can handle popcorn, butter hands and press into balls of uniform size. Place on waxed paper to set.

YIELD: 8 POPCORN BALLS

Kids' Table Turtle Salads

2 drops green food coloring

4 pear halves, in juice from can

16 pecan halves

4 green olives

8 whole cloves

In large bowl, put food coloring in juice from canned pears. Stir. Place pear halves in juice until they turn green. On salad plate, place pear half. Use pecan halves for legs, olives for heads. Stick cloves in olives for eyes.

YIELD: 4 SERVINGS

Indoor S'mores

⅔ cup light corn syrup

2 tablespoons butter

1 (12 ounce) package chocolate chips

1 teaspoon vanilla

1 (10 ounce) package graham crackers, coarsely crumbled

3 cups miniature marshmallows

In 3-quart saucepan, heat corn syrup, butter, and chocolate chips to boiling. Remove from heat. Stir in vanilla. Place graham crackers in large bowl. Pour chocolate mixture over crackers. Stir to coat. Fold in marshmallows, 1 cup at a time. Press into buttered 13x9-inch pan. Let stand until firm.

YIELD: 20 SERVINGS

Santa's Salted Nutty Bars

1 (12 ounce) package peanut butter chips

3 tablespoons butter

1 (14 ounce) can sweetened condensed milk

1 (10 ounce) package miniature marshmallows

2¼ cups roasted nuts

In large saucepan, melt peanut butter chips, butter, and milk over medium heat. Add marshmallows and nuts. Press mixture into buttered 13x9-inch pan. Refrigerate for 2 hours. Cut into squares.

YIELD: 36 SERVINGS

Young Chef's Turkey Sandwiches

2 cups chopped turkey

½ cup mayonnaise

½ cup shredded carrot

¼ cup raisins

¼ cup chopped roasted peanuts

4 sandwich rolls

4 lettuce leaves

Combine turkey, mayonnaise, carrot, raisins, and peanuts. Stir well. Spread turkey mixture evenly on rolls. Top with lettuce. Wrap in plastic wrap and chill for 1 hour.

YIELD: 4 SANDWICHES

Fancy Fruit and Cream

1 (8 ounce) carton sour cream

¼ cup sugar

2 teaspoons vanilla

1½ cups whipped topping

1 cup light corn syrup

1 cup orange juice

1 cinnamon stick

3 large peaches, peeled, pitted, and
   cut into quarters

4 cups strawberries, cut in half

2 cups raspberries

2 cups blueberries

In small bowl, combine sour cream, sugar, vanilla, and whipped topping. Cover with plastic wrap and chill for 2 hours. In large saucepan, combine corn syrup, orange juice, and cinnamon stick. Bring to boil. Boil without stirring for 15 minutes. Reduce heat to simmer. Add peaches. Cook for 4 minutes. Remove from heat. Remove cinnamon stick. Stir in berries. Pour into large bowl. Cover and chill for 2 hours. Just before serving, top fruit mixture with sour cream mixture.

Yield: 6 servings

Cheesy Chicken Casserole

2 (10 ounce) packages frozen broccoli, cooked

2 cups milk

2 (8 ounce) packages cream cheese

1 teaspoon salt

1 teaspoon garlic salt

1½ cups shredded Parmesan cheese, divided

6 chicken breasts, cooked and cut into chunks

Preheat oven to 350 degrees. Place broccoli evenly in bottom of lightly greased 2-quart oblong casserole dish. In heavy saucepan, blend milk, cream cheese, salt, and garlic salt. Stir over low heat until melted and smooth. Stir in half of Parmesan cheese until melted. Pour 1 cup of mixture over broccoli. Spread chicken over top. Cover with remaining cheese mixture. Top with remaining ¾ cup Parmesan cheese. Bake for 30 minutes. Remove from oven and let stand for 10 minutes.

YIELD: 6 SERVINGS

Vanilla Wafer Cake

1 (12 ounce) package vanilla wafers, crushed

2 tablespoons flour

1 teaspoon baking powder

1 cup butter

1 cup sugar

6 eggs

1½ cups milk

2 cups sweetened flaked coconut

2 cups chopped pecans

2 teaspoons vanilla

Preheat oven to 300 degrees. In medium bowl, mix vanilla wafers, flour, and baking powder. Set aside. In large bowl, cream butter and sugar. Add eggs one at a time, beating well after each addition. Add half of crumb mixture, then half of milk. Add remaining crumb mixture and then remaining milk. Add coconut, pecans, and vanilla. Pour into greased tube or Bundt pan and bake for 70 minutes.

YIELD: 12 SERVINGS

Elegant Gelatin Salad

1 (6 ounce) package raspberry gelatin

2 cups boiling water

2 bananas

2 oranges

3 slices canned pineapple

1 cup whipped topping

Dissolve gelatin in boiling water. Let cool. Peel bananas and oranges. Slice crosswise in circles. Cut pineapple into small pieces. Add fruit to cooled gelatin mixture. Pour into mold and refrigerate until firm. Just before serving, turn gelatin out of mold onto serving dish. Spread whipped topping on top.

YIELD: 6 SERVINGS

Choc'laty Sauce

1½ cups sugar

1 cup cocoa

⅛ teaspoon salt

1 cup water

1 teaspoon vanilla

In saucepan, mix together sugar, cocoa, salt, and water. Bring to boil over medium heat, stirring constantly. Boil for 15 minutes, stirring occasionally. Remove from heat. Cool. Stir in vanilla.

YIELD: 1 CUP

Apple Crunch

8 medium apples

½ cup sugar

1 teaspoon cinnamon

1 teaspoon nutmeg

½ cup water

1 cup flour

½ cup brown sugar

½ cup butter

½ cup chopped pecans

Preheat oven to 400 degrees. Wash apples and cut each into 4 pieces. Peel and cut out cores. Cut into thin slices. Place in lightly buttered baking dish. In small bowl, combine sugar, cinnamon, and nutmeg. Sprinkle over apple slices. Pour water evenly over apples. In medium bowl, combine flour, brown sugar, and butter. Cut in butter until crumbly. Add pecans. Spread flour mixture over apples. Bake for 20 minutes. Reduce heat to 350 degrees. Bake for another 25 minutes.

Yield: 8 servings

Honey French Toast

12 slices french bread

6 eggs

1 (12 ounce) can evaporated milk

⅔ cup honey, separate out ¼ cup

1 teaspoon vanilla

½ teaspoon salt

1 tablespoon powdered sugar

½ cup pancake syrup

1 teaspoon cinnamon

Arrange bread slices flat in 13x9-inch baking pan. Combine eggs, milk, ¼ cup honey, vanilla, and salt. Blend well. Pour over bread, turning bread to coat both sides. Cover with plastic wrap and chill overnight. Preheat oven to 400 degrees. Place bread slices on 15x10-inch baking pan. Bake for 15 minutes. Turn slices over and bake for 10 minutes. Remove from oven and sprinkle with powdered sugar. While toast is baking, combine remaining honey, syrup, and cinnamon in saucepan. Bring to boil. Simmer for 5 minutes. Serve honey-syrup mixture with french toast.

YIELD: 6 SERVINGS

Recipe:..
INGREDIENTS:...
....
....

DIRECTIONS:...
....
....
....
....

YIELD:..

Recipe:..
INGREDIENTS:...
....
....

DIRECTIONS:...
....
....
....
....

YIELD:..

Recipe:

INGREDIENTS:

DIRECTIONS:

YIELD:

Recipe:

INGREDIENTS:

DIRECTIONS:

YIELD:

Recipe:

INGREDIENTS:

DIRECTIONS:

YIELD:

On the ninth day of Christmas my true love sent to me:

Nine Main Dishes a-Mixing

Christmas is most truly Christmas when
we celebrate it by giving the light of
love to those who need it most.

RUTH CARTER STAPLETON

Lord, we are nothing without You. Only when we are touched by Your hand of loving-kindness do we find ourselves able to love and cherish ourselves and others. Thank You for the joys of Christmas. Amen.

The shepherds returned, glorifying and praising God for all the things they had heard and seen, which were just as they had been told.

LUKE 2:20 NIV

Ham and Asparagus Rolls *

6 slices deli ham, thin enough to roll, thick enough to hold together

24 large asparagus spears, cooked

2 tablespoons butter, melted

¼ cup butter

⅓ cup flour

1 teaspoon salt

2 teaspoons minced onion

2 cups milk

½ cup shredded cheddar cheese

Preheat oven to 350 degrees. Lay out ham slices on cutting board. Place 4 asparagus spears on each slice. Brush with melted butter and roll up. Place in shallow baking pan. In saucepan, melt ¼ cup butter over flour and salt. Blend in onion and milk gradually. Cook medium heat until thick, stirring constantly. Add cheese and mix well. Pour over ham rolls. Bake for 25 minutes.

Yield: 6 servings

Chicken Tetrazzini *

1 cup shredded Parmesan cheese, divided

1 (10.75 ounce) can cream of mushroom soup

1 (15 ounce) jar Alfredo sauce

1 (3.5 ounce) can sliced mushrooms, drained

½ cup slivered almonds, toasted

½ cup chicken broth

¼ cup dry cooking sherry

½ teaspoon salt

¼ teaspoon pepper

3 cups chopped cooked chicken

7 ounces vermicelli, cooked

Preheat oven to 350 degrees. In large bowl, combine ½ cup Parmesan cheese, soup, Alfredo sauce, mushrooms, almonds, chicken broth, sherry, salt, and pepper. Stir in chicken and pasta. Pour into lightly greased 11x8-inch casserole dish. Sprinkle with remaining ½ cup Parmesan cheese and bake for 30 minutes.

Yield: 8 servings

Sangria Ham *

2 cups brown sugar
1 bone-in butt portion ham
Whole cloves

2 cups sangria
1 cup pineapple juice

Preheat oven to 325 degrees. Pack brown sugar over exterior of ham. Stick in cloves all over. Place ham in roaster pan. Mix together sangria and pineapple juice and pour over meat. Bake for 3 hours, basting every hour. Slice ham and pour cooking juices over slices to serve.

YIELD: 12 TO 15 SERVINGS

Sherried Chicken

¼ cup butter
½ teaspoon salt
¼ teaspoon pepper
6 boneless, skinless chicken breasts
1 (10.75 ounce) can cream of mushroom soup
½ cup cooking sherry

1 (4 ounce) can sliced mushrooms
1 cup water chestnuts, drained
2 tablespoons chopped green bell pepper
½ teaspoon thyme
6 cups cooked rice

Preheat oven to 350 degrees. In large sauté pan, melt butter. Salt and pepper chicken breasts. Place in sauté pan and cook until brown. Transfer chicken breasts to 11x9-inch baking pan, leaving drippings in sauté pan. To sauté pan, add soup, sherry, mushrooms, water chestnuts, bell pepper, and thyme. Mix well. Pour over chicken breasts. Cover and bake for 25 minutes. Uncover and bake for another 14 minutes. Serve over heated rice.

YIELD: 6 SERVINGS

"Day after Christmas" Ham and Sweet Potato Casserole

1½ cups diced cooked ham

1 tablespoon butter

6 cups cooked sweet potatoes

2 eggs, beaten

½ cup milk

1½ tablespoons lemon juice

½ teaspoon salt

Preheat oven to 350 degrees. In large skillet, brown ham slightly in butter. Whip potatoes until smooth and combine with beaten eggs, milk, lemon juice, and salt. Whip thoroughly. Transfer into pan with ham. Mix thoroughly. Spoon into buttered 11x9-inch baking pan. Bake for 45 minutes.

YIELD: 5 SERVINGS

Old England Chops and Apples

5 thick-cut pork chops (about 2 pounds)

6 medium tart apples, cored and sliced 1 inch thick

¼ cup water

½ teaspoon salt

¼ cup sugar

Preheat oven to 350 degrees. Wipe chops with damp cloth. In hot, greased ovenproof skillet, brown chops slowly but well on both sides. Arrange apples on top of chops. Add water; sprinkle lightly with salt and sugar. Cover and bake for 45 to 60 minutes or until tender.

YIELD: 5 SERVINGS

Crabmeat Cakes

3 tablespoons butter

1 clove garlic, peeled and chopped

4 tablespoons flour

1 cup milk

¾ teaspoon salt

⅛ teaspoon pepper

½ teaspoon Worcestershire sauce

1⅔ cups flaked crabmeat

¾ cup dry bread crumbs

1 egg, beaten

2 tablespoons butter

¼ cup milk

1 egg, hard-boiled and chopped

In medium skillet, heat butter and garlic. Remove garlic when butter is melted. Blend in flour and add milk, stirring constantly until sauce boils and thickens. Add salt, pepper, and Worcestershire. Remove from heat. In medium bowl, combine crabmeat with half of bread crumbs and half of sauce. Mix well. Cover tightly and chill. When thoroughly chilled, shape mixture into 10 small patties. Dip patties into remaining bread crumbs, then beaten egg, and again in crumbs. Pan fry in hot skillet with 2 tablespoons butter until browned. Combine remaining sauce with milk and hard-boiled egg. Heat and pour over patties.

YIELD: 5 SERVINGS

Peachy Pecan Ham

1 (2½ pound) cured ham

1 cup peach preserves, divided

1 (11.5 ounce) can peach nectar

1 tablespoon cornstarch

1 teaspoon dry mustard

½ cup packed brown sugar

½ cup chopped pecans

2 large fresh peaches, peeled and sliced

Preheat oven to 325 degrees. Place ham in shallow roasting pan. Score ham, cover, and bake for 45 minutes. Uncover ham and brush with ½ cup peach preserves. Bake for 30 minutes, basting occasionally. In small saucepan, combine peach nectar, cornstarch, and mustard. Stir until smooth. Add remaining ½ cup preserves and brown sugar. Cook over medium heat, stirring constantly until thickened. Stir in pecans and peaches. Cook for 1 minute. Slice ham and serve with peach sauce.

YIELD: 6 TO 8 SERVINGS

Quick Cranberry Barbeque

½ cup chopped onion

2 tablespoons butter, melted

1 cup ketchup

½ cup canned whole cranberry sauce

¼ cup packed brown sugar

3 tablespoons vinegar

1 tablespoon Worcestershire sauce

1 tablespoon mustard

2 cups chicken or ham, cut into julienne strips

6 servings of rice, cooked

In large skillet, sauté onion in butter until tender. Stir in ketchup, cranberry sauce, brown sugar, vinegar, Worcestershire, mustard, and meat. Simmer, uncovered, for 15 minutes. Serve over hot rice.

YIELD: 6 SERVINGS

Holiday Ham Balls

3 cups ground cooked ham

¼ cup butter, melted

1 cup dry bread crumbs

2 eggs, well beaten

½ cup milk

½ cup packed brown sugar

½ teaspoon dry mustard

¼ cup vinegar

¼ cup water

1 tablespoon cornstarch

1 tablespoon water

Preheat oven to 350 degrees. In large bowl, combine ham, butter, bread crumbs, eggs, and milk. Shape into 12 balls. Place in lightly greased baking dish. In small saucepan, combine brown sugar, mustard, vinegar, and ¼ cup water. Cook over low heat, stirring constantly, until sugar dissolves completely. Pour over ham balls. Bake for 30 minutes. Remove from pan. Dissolve cornstarch in 1 tablespoon water. Stir with pan drippings until sauce thickens. Pour over ham balls before serving.

YIELD: 6 SERVINGS

Gingery London Broil

½ cup dark corn syrup

¼ cup soy sauce

2 tablespoons cider vinegar

2 teaspoons ginger

2 cloves garlic, sliced

3 pounds London broil beef, 2 inches thick

In shallow baking dish, stir together corn syrup, soy sauce, vinegar, ginger, and garlic. Add beef, turning to coat. Cover and chill overnight, basting at least once. Grill or broil for 25 minutes, turning and basting frequently. Slice diagonally across grain.

YIELD: 6 TO 8 SERVINGS

Leftover Turkey Stew

1 (16 ounce) can whole tomatoes

2 tablespoons corn oil

1 cup sliced onion

1 clove garlic, minced

½ cup chicken broth

¼ cup dark corn syrup

½ teaspoon thyme

½ teaspoon salt

3 cups cubed cooked turkey

1 (10 ounce) package frozen peas

1 piece orange peel

1 tablespoon cornstarch

3 tablespoons water

Drain tomatoes, reserving liquid, and cut in half. In large skillet, heat oil over medium heat. Add onion and garlic. Sauté for 5 minutes. Stir in tomatoes and liquid, chicken broth, corn syrup, thyme, and salt. Bring to boil. Reduce heat. Simmer for 15 minutes. Add turkey, peas, and orange peel. Simmer for 15 minutes. Dissolve cornstarch in water. Stir into turkey mixture, stirring constantly. Bring to boil. Boil for 1 minute.

YIELD: 6 SERVINGS

Winter Beef Stew

¼ cup corn oil

2 pounds stew beef, cut in 1½-inch cubes

1½ cups chopped onion

1½ cups dry cooking wine

½ cup dark corn syrup

1½ teaspoons salt

½ teaspoon thyme

½ teaspoon marjoram

¼ teaspoon cinnamon

2 sweet potatoes, peeled and sliced ½ inch thick

1 teaspoon grated lemon rind

1 large apple, cut in eighths

2 tablespoons cornstarch

¼ cup water

In 5-quart dutch oven, heat oil over medium heat. Add ½ of beef and brown on all sides. Remove and brown remaining beef. Set aside. Add onion. Sauté for 5 minutes. Reduce heat. Stir in cooking wine, corn syrup, salt, thyme, marjoram, and cinnamon. Add beef. Bring to boil. Reduce heat. Cover and simmer until meat is almost tender. Add potatoes and lemon rind. Cover and simmer for 15 minutes, stirring occasionally. Add apple and simmer for 15 minutes. Dissolve cornstarch in water. Stir into beef mixture. Stir constantly over medium heat until juices come to boil. Boil for 1 minute.

YIELD: 8 SERVINGS

Happy New Year Brisket

1 (5 pound) beef brisket

2 teaspoons garlic salt

1 teaspoon onion salt

2 teaspoons celery salt

1 medium onion, minced

5 tablespoons liquid smoke

1 teaspoon seasoned salt

¼ cup Worcestershire sauce

¼ teaspoon pepper

Arrange brisket in greased 13x9-inch baking dish, fat side down. Sprinkle with garlic salt, onion salt, celery salt, onion, liquid smoke, and seasoned salt. Cover with foil and refrigerate overnight. In the morning, preheat oven to 275 degrees. Sprinkle brisket with Worcestershire and pepper. Re-cover with foil. Bake for 1 hour. Lower heat to 250 degrees and bake for 5 hours. Remove from sauce. Cool slightly and slice or chop.

Yield: 8 to 10 servings

Garlic Leg of Lamb

1 (6 pound) leg of lamb

2 tablespoons butter, softened

2 slices bacon, finely chopped

¼ cup minced parsley

1 tablespoon vinegar

4 cloves garlic, minced

1 teaspoon salt

1 teaspoon paprika

⅛ teaspoon pepper

Score fat of lamb in diamond pattern. In small bowl, combine butter, bacon, parsley, vinegar, garlic, salt, paprika, and pepper. Rub mixture into scored slits and over entire surface of lamb. Cover and chill for 1 hour. Preheat oven to 325 degrees. Place leg of lamb in greased shallow baking pan. Bake for 2½ hours.

YIELD: 8 SERVINGS

Glorious Golden Game Hens

¾ pound pitted dates

Hot water

2 tablespoons Dijon mustard

1 teaspoon salt

4 Cornish game hens

2 tablespoons butter, melted

¼ teaspoon saffron

2 egg yolks, beaten

Preheat oven to 275 degrees. Soak dates for 2 minutes in hot water to soften. Cut into 4 pieces. In small bowl, combine dates with mustard and salt. Rinse each hen and pat dry. Stuff with date mixture. Arrange hens in greased large baking dish. Bake for 50 minutes, basting with butter occasionally. Remove from oven. Combine saffron with egg yolks. Paint hens with mixture. Raise heat to 400 degrees. Bake for 10 minutes or until golden.

YIELD: 4 SERVINGS

Ham and Pineapple Kabobs

½ cup spicy barbeque sauce

¼ cup orange marmalade

1 pound ham, cut into 1-inch cubes

2 (8 ounce) cans pineapple chunks

2 medium green bell peppers, cut into 1-inch pieces

8 wooden skewers

In small bowl, stir together barbeque sauce and marmalade. Reserve ½ of mixutre for basting. Alternate ham, pineapple chunks, and bell peppers on skewers. Place on grill or broiler pan. Brush with ½ of sauce, coating completely. Rotate kabobs ¼ turn every 2 minutes, brushing each time with sauce, until thoroughly heated. Serve with remaining sauce.

Yield: 8 servings

Chicken á la King

1½ cups fresh mushroom caps

5 tablespoons butter

6 tablespoons chopped green bell pepper

1 tablespoon capers

1 teaspoon salt

¼ teaspoon paprika

2 cups diced cooked chicken

2½ tablespoons flour

2 tablespoons butter

3 cups thin cream

2 egg yolks

In large skillet, sauté mushrooms in butter for 5 minutes. Add bell pepper, capers, salt, paprika, and chicken. In saucepan, create white sauce by dissolving flour in butter and adding cream. When sauce is thickened and bubbling, add egg yolks. Stir well. Pour over chicken mixture. Heat thoroughly.

Yield: 5 servings

Rockin' Roast Beef Sandwiches

6 kaiser rolls, split

2 eggs, beaten

2 tablespoons coarse salt

1 cup chopped sweet onion

1 tablespoon olive oil

1 tablespoon butter

4 cups beef broth

½ cup dry white wine

1 tablespoon chopped garlic

1 tablespoon tomato paste

2 teaspoons minced thyme

1½ pounds leftover or deli roast beef, thinly sliced

Horseradish and jus sauce

Preheat oven to 375 degrees. Place rolls on cookie sheet. Brush rolls with eggs. Sprinkle with salt. Bake for 5 minutes. Sauté onion in oil and butter. Add broth, wine, garlic, tomato paste, and thyme. Over medium heat, simmer for 15 minutes. Turn off heat. Strain. Return to pan. Add roast beef to warm. Arrange beef on rolls. Serve with horseradish and jus sauce.

Yield: 4 servings

Festive Flounder Marinara

1 cup sliced onion

2 tablespoons butter

2 tablespoons flour

1 (1 pound) can stewed tomatoes

½ teaspoon basil

16 ounces frozen flounder fillets

¼ cup grated Parmesan cheese

Preheat oven to 375 degrees. In ovenproof skillet, sauté onion in butter for 5 minutes over medium heat, stirring constantly. Remove from heat. Stir in flour, stewed tomatoes, and basil. Mix until smooth. Slice frozen fillets in 6 pieces. Place in sauce. Sprinkle with Parmesan cheese. Bake in covered skillet for 10 minutes. Remove cover. Bake 6 minutes longer or until golden brown.

Yield: 6 servings

Recipe:...

INGREDIENTS:
....
....
....

DIRECTIONS:
....
....
....
....
....

YIELD:

Recipe:...

INGREDIENTS:
....
....

DIRECTIONS:
....
....
....
....

YIELD:

Recipe:

INGREDIENTS:

DIRECTIONS:

YIELD:

Recipe:

INGREDIENTS:

DIRECTIONS:

YIELD:

Recipe:

INGREDIENTS:

DIRECTIONS:

YIELD:

On the tenth day of Christmas my true love sent to me:

Ten Salads a-Crunching

Bless us, Lord, this Christmas, with quietness
of mind; teach us to be patient and always to be kind.

HELEN STEINER RICE

Father, thank You for opening our eyes to see You—
really know You. To know You is to love You.
To spend time with You is to be energized
and renewed. This is Your gift to us. Amen.

*God said, "I give you every seed-bearing plant on the
face of the whole earth and every tree that has fruit
with seed in it. They will be yours for food."*

Genesis 1:29 niv

Mandarin Orange Salad *

❦ ⊱⊰ ❦ ⊱⊰ ❦ ⊱⊰ ❦ ❦

2 small packages orange gelatin

1 cup boiling water

2 cups orange sherbet

1 (15 ounce) can mandarin oranges, drained

1 cup heavy cream, whipped

Dissolve gelatin in boiling water. Stir in sherbet until melted. Chill until thick and cool but not set, then fold in oranges and whipped cream. Pour into mold or serving bowl and let set in refrigerator for 2 hours.

Yield: 8 servings

Holiday Fruit Medley

½ cup french dressing

2 tablespoons brown sugar

¼ teaspoon cinnamon

½ cup fresh pineapple chunks

1 peach, peeled and sliced

2 kiwi, peeled and sliced

1 cup cantaloupe chunks

½ cup strawberry halves

8 thin pineapple slices, peeled

8 thin cantaloupe slices, peeled

Stir together dressing, brown sugar, and cinnamon until smooth. Toss pineapple chunks, peach slices, kiwi slices, cantaloupe chunks, and strawberries with dressing. Arrange remaining fruit on serving dish. Arrange marinated fruit on top.

Yield: 6 servings

Snowy Grapefruit and Shrimp Mold

1 (1 pound) can grapefruit sections in syrup

3 cups grapefruit juice

2 (.25 ounce) envelopes unflavored gelatin

¼ cup sugar

¼ teaspoon salt

1½ cups cooked shrimp

½ cup finely diced celery

¼ cup powdered sugar

Drain grapefruit sections, reserving ½ cup syrup. In medium bowl, combine reserved syrup with grapefruit juice. In large saucepan, mix together gelatin, sugar, and salt. Add 1 cup grapefruit juice mixture. Cook over low heat, stirring constantly, until gelatin and sugar dissolve. Remove from heat. Add remaining grapefruit juice mixture. Place several whole grapefruit sections and several whole shrimp in bottom of 6-cup mold. Cover with small amount of gelatin mixture and chill until firm. Chill remaining gelatin until it has consistency of unbeaten egg white. Cut remaining shrimp into small pieces and remaining grapefruit sections in half. Fold into gelatin along with celery. Spoon on top of firm first layer. Chill again to firm. Invert on serving plate and sift sugar on top.

YIELD: 8 TO 10 SERVINGS

Merry Christmas Cranberry Freeze

3 cups cranberries, finely chopped

1½ cups sugar

1 (8.5 ounce) can crushed pineapple, undrained

½ cup chopped walnuts

1 (8 ounce) package cream cheese, softened

2 cups whipped topping

Mix together cranberries, sugar, pineapple, and walnuts. Gradually add cream cheese, mixing well. Fold in whipped topping. Pour into 1½-quart bowl or lightly greased 6½-cup ring mold. Freeze until firm.

YIELD: 8 TO 10 SERVINGS

Christmas Red Tuna Salad

4 beets, cooked, peeled, and cubed

1 (7 ounce) can tuna, drained and flaked

1 tart apple, cored and cubed

1 stalk celery, chopped

3½ tablespoons mayonnaise

2 tablespoons lemon juice

¼ teaspoon dill weed

In medium bowl, combine beets, tuna, apple, celery, mayonnaise, lemon juice, and dill weed. Toss thoroughly and chill until ready to serve.

YIELD: 4 SERVINGS

Golden Holiday Salad

1 cup unsweetened pineapple juice

2 tablespoons unflavored gelatin

⅛ cup cold water

⅓ cup honey

¾ cup orange juice

¼ cup lemon juice

1 cup coarsely grated carrot

1 cup cut-up orange segments

1½ cups crushed pineapple, drained

⅔ cup chopped pecans or walnuts

In medium saucepan, heat pineapple juice until hot. In cup, soften gelatin in water. Then dissolve in pineapple juice. Stir in honey and blend well. Add orange juice and lemon juice. Pour into serving bowl and chill until mixture begins to thicken. Fold in carrot, orange segments, pineapple, and nuts. Chill until firm. Continue to chill until ready to serve.

YIELD: 6 SERVINGS

Elegant Snowberries Salad

2 cups water, divided

3 cups fresh cranberries, divided

1 cup sugar

2 (.25 ounce) envelopes unflavored
  gelatin

½ cup water

1 (12 ounce) bottle ginger ale

1 cup peeled, cored, and diced pear

1 cup seedless green grapes, halved

½ cup diced celery

½ cup chopped walnuts

1 egg white, beaten

1 cup sugar

In medium saucepan, combine 1½ cups water, 2 cups cranberries, and 1 cup sugar. Bring to boil. Reduce heat and simmer uncovered for 2 minutes or until berries pop. Sprinkle gelatin in ½ cup water. Let stand for 1 minute. Add to cranberry mixture. Cook over medium heat, stirring constantly, until gelatin dissolves. Add ginger ale, stirring well. Cover and chill for 2 hours. Fold pear, grapes, celery, and walnuts into gelatin mixture. Spoon gelatin into lightly greased 8-cup ring mold. Cover and chill until firm. Place 1 cup cranberries on waxed paper. Brush with beaten egg white on all sides. Sprinkle with 1 cup sugar. Let dry completely. Turn mold onto serving place. Sprinkle cranberries around sides.

Yield: 12 servings

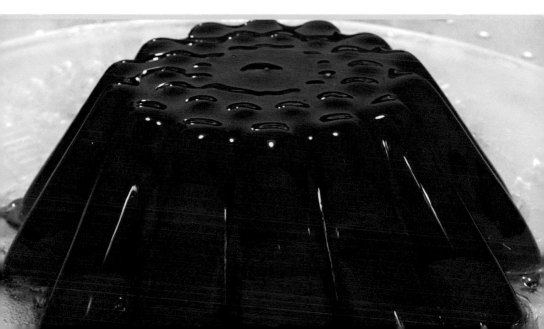

Strawberry and Spinach Salad

8 cups torn spinach

3 kiwi, peeled, sliced, and divided

1 cup fresh strawberries, halved and divided

¾ cup coarsely chopped macadamia nuts or pecans, divided

2 tablespoons strawberry jam

2 tablespoons cider vinegar

⅓ cup salad oil

In large bowl, combine spinach, half of kiwi slices, half of strawberries, and half of nuts. Set aside. Combine jam and vinegar in blender. With blender running, gradually add oil in slow, steady stream. Process until blended. Right before serving, pour dressing over spinach mixture and toss. Divide spinach mixture evenly on 8 salad plates. Top evenly with remaining fruit and nuts.

Yield: 8 servings

North Pole Fresh Fruit Bowl

1 cup sugar

1 cup water

¼ cup lemon juice

1 cup sliced plums

1 cup seedless grapes

1 cup sliced nectarines

1 cup diced pears

1 cup sliced peaches

1 cup strawberry halves

2 cups whipped topping

½ cup chopped walnuts

½ cup toasted flaked coconut

In 2-quart saucepan, combine sugar and water. Bring to boil, stirring until sugar dissolves. Boil rapidly for 5 minutes. Cool completely. Stir in lemon juice. In large serving bowl, combine plums, grapes, nectarines, pears, peaches, and strawberries. Add syrup and stir gently. Cover and refrigerate until ready to serve. Just before serving, add whipped topping and sprinkle walnuts and coconut on top.

YIELD: 12 SERVINGS

Sautéed Mushroom Salad

1 pound fresh mushrooms, sliced

1 medium onion, sliced

1 green bell pepper, cut into strips

1 tablespoon butter

2 tablespoons soy sauce

5 lettuce cups

4 slices bacon, cooked and crumbled

Sauté mushrooms, onion, and bell pepper in butter until tender. Stir in soy sauce. Spoon mixture into lettuce cups. Sprinkle bacon over salad cups.

YIELD: 5 SERVINGS

Luscious Lettuce and Brie Salad

1 head curly endive, torn

1 head iceberg lettuce, torn

1 head romaine lettuce, torn

10 ounces fully ripened Brie

1 cup olive oil

½ cup white wine vinegar

2 teaspoons lemon juice

1 tablespoon plus 1 teaspoon Dijon mustard

2 large cloves garlic, minced

1 teaspoon minced green onions

¼ teaspoon pepper

½ cup garlic-flavored croutons

In large salad bowl, combine endive and lettuces. Toss well. Set aside. Remove rind from Brie. Cut cheese into small pieces. In large skillet, combine Brie, oil, vinegar, lemon juice, mustard, garlic, green onions, and pepper. Cook over medium heat, stirring constantly, until cheese melts. When ready to serve, pour warm dressing over greens, tossing gently to coat evenly. Sprinkle with croutons.

YIELD: 18 SERVINGS

Santa's Swiss Cheese Salad

½ cup mayonnaise

2 tablespoons Dijon mustard

½ teaspoon pepper

½ teaspoon celery seed

½ pound swiss cheese, cut into strips

1 cup chopped celery

1 small onion, thinly sliced

4 large lettuce leaves

In small bowl, combine mayonnaise, mustard, pepper, and celery seed. In large bowl, combine cheese, celery, and onion. Add mayonnaise mixture. Line salad bowl with lettuce leaves. Pour into bowl when ready to serve.

YIELD: 4 SERVINGS

Black-Eyed Pea Salad

2 (16 ounce) cans black-eyed peas,
    rinsed and drained

¼ cup diced celery

1 small sweet red bell pepper, diced

2 tablespoons minced fresh cilantro

3 tablespoons olive oil

2 tablespoons soy sauce

1 tablespoon red wine vinegar or
    balsamic vinegar

In large serving bowl, combine black-eyed peas, celery, bell pepper, and cilantro.
In measuring cup, combine oil, soy sauce, and vinegar. Pour over salad and toss.
Cover with plastic wrap and let stand for 1 hour before serving.

Yield: 4 servings

Apple and Peanut Salad

5 medium sweet apples, unpeeled, cored, and quartered

1 tablespoon lemon juice

4 stalks celery

½ cup mayonnaise

½ cup coarsely chopped peanuts

⅓ teaspoon paprika

In large bowl, cut apples into ½-inch cubes and sprinkle with lemon juice. Cut celery into thin crosswise slices. Combine celery and mayonnaise with apples and toss lightly. Just before serving, add peanuts. Stir gently. Garnish with paprika.

YIELD: 5 SERVINGS

Sensational Shrimp Salad

2 cups cleaned, cooked shrimp, chilled

½ cup sliced celery, chilled

1 teaspoon minced onion

⅓ cup mayonnaise

¼ cup chili sauce

3 tablespoons lemon juice

5 large lettuce leaves

3 hard-boiled eggs, chilled

In medium bowl, combine shrimp, celery, onion, mayonnaise, chili sauce, and lemon juice. Return to refrigerator. When ready to serve, line salad plates with lettuce leaves. Slice eggs lengthwise and arrange in ring on top of lettuce. Spoon salad mixture into center of each ring.

YIELD: 5 SERVINGS

My Favorite Christmas Salad Recipes

Recipe: ....

INGREDIENTS: ....

....

....

DIRECTIONS: ....

....

....

....

....

YIELD: ....

Recipe: ....

INGREDIENTS: ....

....

DIRECTIONS: ....

....

....

....

YIELD: ....

Recipe:...

Ingredients:...

....

....

Directions:..

....

....

....

....

Yield:...

Recipe:...

Ingredients:...

....

....

Directions:..

....

....

....

....

Yield:...

Recipe:...

Ingredients:...

....

....

Directions:..

....

....

....

....

Yield:...

On the eleventh day of Christmas my true love sent to me:

Eleven Sides a-Steaming

*The Word who found a dwelling in Mary's womb
comes to knock on the heart of every person
with singular intensity this Christmas.*

POPE JOHN PAUL II

Jesus, fill our hearts this Christmas with more love than we can hold. Fill us to overflowing so that we can spill Your love on others. Amen.

To us a child is born, to us a son is given,
and the government will be on his shoulders.
And he will be called Wonderful Counselor,
Mighty God, Everlasting Father, Prince of Peace.

Isaiah 9:6 niv

Sweet Potato Casserole *

6 cups cooked and mashed
  sweet potatoes

1 cup sugar

1 teaspoon salt

4 eggs, beaten

½ cup butter, melted

1 cup milk

1 teaspoon cinnamon

1 cup brown sugar

⅓ cup flour

⅓ cup butter

1 cup chopped nuts

Preheat oven to 350 degrees. In large bowl, combine sweet potatoes, sugar, salt, eggs, butter, milk, and cinnamon. Pour into greased 13x9-inch pan. In medium bowl, combine brown sugar and flour. Cut in butter with pastry blender. Add nuts. Sprinkle evenly over sweet potato mixture. Bake for 1 hour.

Yield: 10 servings

Escalloped Carrots and Potatoes

1 tablespoon flour

1 cup evaporated milk, divided

1 cup water

2 teaspoons salt

½ teaspoon pepper

6 medium carrots, peeled and sliced

1 small onion, sliced

1 pound potatoes, pared and sliced

2 tablespoons butter

Preheat oven to 350 degrees. In large heavy saucepan, blend flour with 1 tablespoon milk to make smooth paste. Add remaining milk and water. Stir until smooth and cook over direct heat, stirring constantly, until sauce boils and thickens. Add salt and pepper. Add carrots, onion, and potatoes. Bring to boil again. Turn into buttered 8-cup casserole dish. Dot with butter. Cover and bake for 30 minutes or until vegetables are tender.

YIELD: 5 SERVINGS

Comet's Carrot Soufflé

5 medium carrots, shredded
(about 2 cups)

3 eggs, separated

2 tablespoons butter

2 tablespoons flour

½ cup milk, divided

1 teaspoon salt

Preheat oven to 325 degrees. In medium saucepan, boil carrots to halfway done. Drain and set aside. In medium bowl, beat egg whites to stiff peaks. In large skillet, over medium heat, melt butter. Add flour and enough milk to make smooth paste. Add remaining milk and salt. Bring to boil. Beat egg yolks in large bowl. Add sauce. Stir vigorously. Fold in carrots. Fold in egg whites. Turn into buttered 4-cup casserole dish and bake for 1 hour. Best when served immediately.

YIELD: 5 SERVINGS

Stuffed Baked Potatoes

5 large baking potatoes of uniform
size and shape

⅔ cup butter

1 teaspoon salt

½ cup hot milk

½ cup shredded American or cheddar
cheese

Preheat oven to 400 degrees. Bake potatoes until soft. Cut in half lengthwise. Scoop out potatoes, reserving skins, and place in medium bowl. Add butter, salt, and hot milk. Mash. Whip with wooden spoon until light and fluffy. Spoon carefully into potato skins. Sprinkle with cheese and return to oven. Use broiler to toast tops of potatoes.

YIELD: 5 SERVINGS

Eggplant Casserole

1 cup shredded cheese, divided

1 cup dry bread crumbs

6 tablespoons butter, divided

5 cups diced eggplant, divided

2 onions, sliced, divided

1 teaspoon salt

¼ teaspoon pepper

3 tomatoes, peeled and diced, or 1½ cups canned tomatoes, divided

Preheat oven to 375 degrees. In measuring cup, combine ¼ cup cheese with bread crumbs. Set aside. In large saucepan, melt 1 tablespoon butter and sauté eggplant slowly for 5 minutes. In large buttered casserole dish, arrange layer of eggplant. Add layer of sliced onions. Sprinkle with salt, pepper, and half of remaining cheese. Add layer of eggplant. Add layer of tomatoes. Season with additional salt and pepper. Sprinkle with rest of cheese. Add any remaining eggplant, onions, or tomatoes. Sprinkle with bread crumb mixture. Dot with remaining 5 tablespoons butter. Bake for 35 minutes or until eggplant is tender.

YIELD: 5 SERVINGS

Easy Potatoes Romanoff

8 medium potatoes, boiled with skins

6 green onions, chopped

2 cups sour cream

2 cups shredded sharp cheddar cheese

⅛ teaspoon salt

⅛ teaspoon pepper

Preheat oven to 350 degrees. Peel potatoes. Dice or grate. In large bowl, combine potatoes, green onions, sour cream, cheese, salt, and pepper. Blend well. Pour into greased 2-quart casserole dish. Bake for 30 minutes.

YIELD: 6 TO 8 SERVINGS

Artichoke Spinach Dish

1 (6 ounce) jar marinated artichoke hearts

2 (20 ounce) packages frozen spinach, thawed and drained

1 (8 ounce) package cream cheese

3 tablespoons butter, softened

4 tablespoons milk

½ cup grated Parmesan cheese

½ teaspoon pepper

Preheat oven to 350 degrees. Place artichokes in 2-quart casserole dish. Spread spinach evenly over artichokes. In small bowl, beat cream cheese and butter until smooth. Add milk. Beat well. Spread over spinach. Sprinkle with Parmesan cheese and pepper. Cover and bake for 30 minutes. Uncover and bake for 10 additional minutes.

Yield: 6 servings

Escalloped Corn

1 (14.75 ounce) can cream-style corn

2 eggs, beaten

½ cup buttery cracker crumbs

¼ cup butter, melted

¼ cup evaporated milk

¼ cup finely shredded carrot

¼ cup chopped green bell pepper

1 tablespoon chopped onion

1 tablespoon chopped celery

6 drops Tabasco sauce

½ teaspoon sugar

½ teaspoon salt

½ cup shredded cheddar cheese

½ teaspoon paprika

Preheat oven to 350 degrees. In large bowl, combine corn, eggs, cracker crumbs, butter, milk, carrot, bell pepper, onion, celery, Tabasco, sugar, salt, and cheese. Pour into buttered 8x8-inch baking pan. Sprinkle with paprika. Bake for 30 minutes or until center is firm.

Yield: 6 servings

Holiday Table Baked Squash

3 pounds yellow squash, sliced, cooked

¾ cup chopped onion

4 teaspoons salt

½ teaspoon pepper

3 tablespoons sugar

2 tablespoons flour

3 eggs, beaten

½ cup butter, melted

1½ cups evaporated milk

½ cup buttery cracker crumbs

Preheat oven to 350 degrees. In large bowl, combine squash, onion, salt, pepper, sugar, flour, eggs, butter, and milk. Mix well. Pour into 1½-quart buttered casserole dish. Sprinkle with cracker crumbs. Bake for 40 minutes.

YIELD: 8 SERVINGS

Garlic Asparagus

1 pound asparagus (10 to 12 stalks)

4 tablespoons olive oil

1 teaspoon garlic vinegar

1 teaspoon minced garlic

¼ teaspoon salt

¼ teaspoon pepper

2 teaspoons water

Preheat oven to 350 degrees. Trim asparagus ends. In small bowl, toss together oil, vinegar, garlic, salt, pepper, and water. Place asparagus in medium baking dish. Pour oil mixture evenly over top. Cover and bake for 10 to 14 minutes.

YIELD: 4 SERVINGS

Carrots and Onion Au Gratin

6 large carrots

1 large onion

2 tablespoons flour

1 teaspoon salt

2 tablespoons butter

1 cup shredded cheddar cheese

½ cup dry bread crumbs

1 cup water

Preheat oven to 325 degrees. Clean and slice carrots and onion. In small bowl, combine flour and salt. Place carrots and onion in layers in greased 1½-quart casserole dish. Sprinkle each layer with flour mixture. Dot with butter. Sprinkle with cheese and bread crumbs. Pour water evenly over top. Cover and bake for 1½ hours or until carrots are tender.

YIELD: 6 SERVINGS

Oranges, Yams, and Coconut

1 (29 ounce) can yams

5 tablespoons butter, divided

2 tablespoons sugar

½ cup fresh orange sections or mandarin orange sections

¼ cup sweetened flaked coconut

½ teaspoon grated lemon rind

Preheat oven to 450 degrees. Drain and mash yams. Add 3 tablespoons butter, sugar, orange sections, coconut, and lemon rind. Spoon into greased 1-quart casserole dish. Dot with remaining 2 tablespoons butter. Bake for 20 minutes.

YIELD: 6 SERVINGS

Celebration Mac and Cheese

1 cup finely chopped green bell
   pepper

¾ cup finely chopped onion

½ cup butter

2 tablespoons flour

1 (12 ounce) can evaporated milk

½ cup milk

4 cups shredded cheddar cheese,
   divided

1 cup American cheese, cubed

⅛ teaspoon pepper

1 (12 ounce) package elbow macaroni,
   cooked and drained

1 tablespoon paprika

Preheat oven to 350 degrees. In large skillet, sauté bell pepper and onion in butter. Add flour and milks, stirring well. Cook for 1 minute, stirring constantly, until thickened. Add 3 cups cheddar cheese, American cheese, and pepper. Stir until melted. Add macaroni to cheese sauce. Stir well. Pour into greased 3-quart baking dish. Bake uncovered for 20 minutes. Sprinkle with remaining 1 cup cheddar cheese and paprika. Bake for 5 minutes or until mixture is hot and bubbly.

Yield: 8 servings

Rich Rice and Pecans

1 pound fresh mushrooms, sliced

4 green onions, sliced

1 clove garlic, minced

½ cup butter, melted

2 cups long-grain brown rice, uncooked

1 teaspoon salt

½ teaspoon thyme

¼ teaspoon pepper

¼ teaspoon turmeric

3¾ cups beef broth, undiluted

2¼ cups water

1½ cups chopped pecans

Preheat oven to 325 degrees. In dutch oven, sauté mushrooms, green onions, and garlic in butter until tender. Add rice. Cook over medium heat for 3 minutes, stirring constantly. Add salt, thyme, pepper, and turmeric. Stir well. Add broth, water, and pecans. Bring to boil. Remove from heat. Cover and bake for 80 minutes or until rice is tender and liquid is absorbed.

Yield: 12 servings

Green Beans with Sweet and Sour Sauce

1½ pounds whole green beans, trimmed

2 onions, cut into rings

6 tablespoons butter

6 tablespoons flour

⅓ cup cider vinegar

¼ cup sugar

⅛ teaspoon salt

In 2-quart saucepan, combine green beans and onions. Cover with water and simmer for 20 minutes. Reserve 2½ cups liquid from beans for sauce. Drain remaining liquid. In medium saucepan, melt butter over low heat. Add flour and stir for 15 minutes or until golden brown. Gradually add reserved liquid, vinegar, and sugar. Stir over medium heat until thick and bubbly. Add salt. Add beans and onions and simmer for 10 minutes.

YIELD: 6 SERVINGS

Fried Spinach Balls

2 cups cooked spinach

2 tablespoons butter, melted

2 eggs, divided and beaten

1½ cups dry bread crumbs, divided

2 tablespoons grated onion

2 tablespoons shredded cheddar cheese

⅛ teaspoon allspice

2 tablespoons water

Fat for frying

Chop spinach. In medium bowl, combine spinach with butter, 1 egg, 1 cup bread crumbs, onion, cheese, and allspice. Stir. Let stand for 10 minutes. Shape into balls. Combine remaining egg with water. Roll spinach balls in remaining ½ cup bread crumbs, then in egg, and again in crumbs. In large skillet, preferably cast iron, fry in deep fat until brown. Drain.

YIELD: 6 SERVINGS

Sausage Mushroom Stuffing

1 pound bulk sausage

2 cups chopped celery

2 cups sliced fresh mushrooms

1½ cups chopped onion

1¼ cups chicken broth

2 (7 ounce) packages herb-seasoned stuffing mix

1½ cups mincemeat

1 cup water chestnuts, coarsely chopped

2 teaspoons poultry seasoning

Preheat oven to 350 degrees. In large skillet, brown sausage. Drain. Add celery, mushrooms, and onion. Cook until onion is tender. Add chicken broth. Bring to boil. In large bowl, combine stuffing mix, mincemeat, water chestnuts, and poultry seasoning. Mix well. Add sausage mixture. Mix well. Transfer to greased 3-quart baking dish. Cover and bake for 45 minutes.

YIELD: 3 QUARTS

Rudolph's Slow Cooker Dressing

1 medium onion, chopped

½ cup chopped celery

2 tablespoons butter

1 (8 inch round) loaf corn bread

8 slices day-old bread

1½ tablespoons poultry seasoning

1 teaspoon salt

½ teaspoon pepper

2 (10.5 ounce) cans cream of chicken soup

2 cups chicken broth

4 eggs, beaten

In small skillet, sauté onion and celery in butter. In large bowl, crumble breads. Add onion and celery mixture, poultry seasoning, salt, pepper, soup, broth, and eggs. Pour into slow cooker. Cook on high for 2 hours or low for 3½ hours.

YIELD: 8 SERVINGS

Aunt Blanche's Scalloped Onions

12 small boiling onions

1 cup diced celery

½ cup sliced almonds, toasted

2 tablespoons grated Parmesan cheese

¼ cup butter

3 tablespoons flour

1 cup milk

½ cup light cream

½ teaspoon salt

⅛ teaspoon pepper

¼ teaspoon paprika

Preheat oven to 350 degrees. In medium saucepan, cover onions and celery with water and boil for 15 minutes or until tender. Drain. Place in lightly greased 2-quart casserole dish. Sprinkle with almonds and Parmesan cheese. Set aside. In heavy saucepan, melt butter over low heat. Add flour, stirring until smooth. Cook for 1 minute, stirring constantly. Gradually add milk and light cream. Cook over medium heat, stirring constantly, until mixture thickens and bubbles. Add salt and pepper. Stir well. Pour sauce over onion mixture. Sprinkle with paprika. Bake for 30 minutes.

Yield: 6 servings

Cauliflower with Raisins

1 small head cauliflower

2 teaspoons minced garlic

¼ cup olive oil

2 tablespoons raisins, plumped

¼ teaspoon salt

⅛ teaspoon pepper

2 tablespoons chopped fresh parsley

Wash cauliflower and leave whole. In dutch oven, boil cauliflower in 4 quarts water for 7 minutes. Drain. Break into florets. In large skillet, sauté garlic in olive oil. Add raisins, cauliflower, salt, and pepper. Cover and cook over low heat for 10 minutes or until tender, stirring occasionally. Sprinkle with parsley.

YIELD: 6 SERVINGS

Fancy Mushrooms and Spinach

18 large fresh mushrooms

1 (10 ounce) package frozen chopped spinach, thawed

¼ cup butter, melted

1 medium onion, minced

1 egg yolk, beaten

¼ cup grated Parmesan cheese, divided

½ teaspoon salt

⅛ teaspoon nutmeg

⅛ teaspoon pepper

Preheat oven to 325 degrees. Remove stems from mushrooms. Finely chop stems. Set aside. Cook spinach and drain well. Dip mushroom caps in melted butter. Place in 13x9-inch baking dish, cap side down. In medium skillet, sauté chopped mushroom stems and onion in remaining butter. Add spinach. Stir well. Set aside. In small bowl, combine egg yolk, 2½ tablespoons cheese, salt, nutmeg, and pepper. Stir well. Add spinach mixture and stir well. Spoon evenly into mushroom caps. Sprinkle with remaining cheese. Bake for 25 minutes.

YIELD: 6 SERVINGS

My Favorite Christmas Side Dish Recipes

Recipe:

INGREDIENTS:

DIRECTIONS:

YIELD:

Recipe:

INGREDIENTS:

DIRECTIONS:

YIELD:

Recipe:...

Ingredients:..

....

....

Directions:...

....

....

....

....

Yield:..

Recipe:...

Ingredients:..

....

....

Directions:...

....

....

....

....

Yield:..

Recipe:...

Ingredients:..

....

....

Directions:...

....

....

....

....

Yield:..

On the twelfth day of Christmas my true love sent to me:

Twelve Soups a-Simmering

May peace be your gift at Christmas
and your blessing all year through.

AUTHOR UNKNOWN

Dear Father, Your greatness reaches to all generations. Your love to every place and time. Your goodness to all without distinction. You are our great and benevolent God. The only One in whom our hearts can fully trust. Amen.

Now to the King eternal, immortal, invisible, the only God, be honor and glory for ever and ever. Amen.

1 TIMOTHY 1:17 NIV

French Onion Soup *

2 onions, roughly chopped

¼ cup butter

1 quart beef stock

1 tablespoon beef stock concentrate

⅛ teaspoon salt

⅛ teaspoon pepper

4 slices french baguette, toasted

1 cup shaved Gruyère cheese

In large skillet, sauté onions in butter until slightly brown and tender. Add beef stock, beef stock concentrate, salt, and pepper. Simmer for 1 hour, uncovered, until reduced by a third. When ready to serve, place one slice of bread in each serving bowl. Pour in hot soup and top generously with cheese. Immediately place bowls on heavy cookie sheet and put under broiler to melt and brown cheese.

YIELD: 4 SERVINGS

Jack Cheese and Onion Soup

2 cups chicken broth

1 cup finely chopped onion

1 cup diced tomatoes

1 (4 ounce) can chopped green chilies, undrained

1 teaspoon minced garlic

¼ cup plus 2 tablespoons butter

¼ cup plus 2 tablespoons flour

5 cups milk, divided

3 cups shredded Monterey Jack cheese

½ teaspoon salt

⅛ teaspoon pepper

In large saucepan, combine broth, onion, tomatoes, chilies, and garlic. Bring to boil. Cover and reduce heat. Simmer for 12 minutes. Remove from heat and set aside. In heavy saucepan, melt butter over low heat. Add flour, stirring until smooth. Cook for 1 minute, stirring constantly. Gradually add 3½ cups milk. Cook over medium heat, stirring constantly until thick and bubbly. Add onion mixture, remaining 1½ cups milk, cheese, salt, and pepper. Cook, stirring constantly, until cheese melts and soup is thoroughly heated.

Yield: 6 servings

Crab Bisque *

8 ounces jumbo lump crabmeat

1 teaspoon salt

⅛ teaspoon pepper

¼ teaspoon thyme

1 bay leaf

1 cup rice, uncooked

½ cup heavy cream

2 tablespoons small croutons

Remove any bones or ligaments from crabmeat. Place crabmeat, salt, pepper, thyme, bay leaf, and rice in 2 quarts boiling water. Cook for 5 minutes. Reduce heat to simmer and cover. Cook for 1 hour. Remove from heat and cool. Shortly before serving, add cream and sprinkle with croutons.

YIELD: 6 SERVINGS

Green Pea Soup

8 cups shredded romaine lettuce

1 (10 ounce) package frozen peas

½ cup sliced green onions

2 cups chicken broth

1½ cups light cream

1 teaspoon sugar

1 teaspoon salt

⅛ teaspoon nutmeg

⅛ teaspoon pepper

8 lemon slices

In 4-quart saucepan, combine lettuce, peas, green onions, and chicken broth. Bring to boil over medium heat. Reduce heat and simmer, covered, for 10 minutes. In blender or food processor, place half of lettuce mixture and liquid. Cover and blend until smooth (about 1 minute). Repeat with remaining lettuce mixture and liquid. Pour back into pan. Add cream, sugar, salt, nutmeg, and pepper. Stir well. Cook over medium heat, stirring constantly, until well blended. Serve in individual bowls with lemon slice on top.

YIELD: 8 SERVINGS

Frosty Christmas Green Avocado Soup

1 medium ripe avocado, peeled and coarsely chopped

2 cups milk

½ cup minced red onion

½ cup chopped green chilies

¼ cup sour cream

½ teaspoon cumin

¼ teaspoon salt

¼ teaspoon black pepper

⅛ teaspoon red pepper

In blender or food processor, process avocado until smooth. In large bowl, combine avocado, milk, onion, chilies, sour cream, cumin, salt, and peppers. Stir well. Cover and chill.

YIELD: 4 CUPS

- -

Frosty Christmas Red Pepper Soup

4 cups chopped leeks

6 large sweet red bell peppers, thinly sliced

1 cup butter, melted

2 tablespoons vegetable oil

3 cups chicken broth

½ teaspoon salt

¼ teaspoon white pepper

6 cups buttermilk

In dutch oven, sauté leeks and bell peppers in butter and oil until tender. Add broth, salt, and pepper. Stir well. Bring to boil. Cover, reduce heat, and simmer for 30 minutes. In blender or food processor, process ⅓ of pepper mixture at a time until smooth. Strain pureed pepper mixture. Let cool slightly before stirring in buttermilk. Cover and chill.

YIELD: 14 CUPS

Thai Broccoli Soup

2 pounds broccoli

3½ cups chicken broth, divided

3 tablespoons butter

2 onions, chopped

1½ teaspoons curry powder

½ cup sour cream

½ cup chopped roasted peanuts

Coarsely chop broccoli stems and cut off florets. Set aside. In large saucepan, bring 1 cup broth to boil. Add ½ of florets. Cook for 4 minutes or until almost tender. Drain, reserving broth. Chill cooked florets. In large saucepan, melt butter. Add onion and curry powder. Sauté until onion is tender. Stir in broccoli stems and remaining florets, reserved broth, and remaining 2½ cups broth. Bring to boil. Cover, reduce heat, and simmer for 12 minutes or until tender. Transfer ½ of broccoli mixture to blender or food processor. Process until smooth. Repeat with remaining broccoli mixture. Pour into bowl, cover, and chill. When ready to serve, pour into individual bowls and add spoonful of sour cream on top. Sprinkle with peanuts.

YIELD: 6 SERVINGS

Curried Carrot Soup

1 pound carrots, pared and sliced

4¼ cups chicken broth

¼ teaspoon salt

⅛ teaspoon pepper

1 medium onion, sliced

2 tablespoons butter

1½ teaspoons curry powder

1½ cups yogurt

8 cucumber slices

½ cup grated carrot

In large saucepan, combine carrots, chicken broth, salt, and pepper. Bring to boil. Reduce heat and simmer for 10 minutes or until carrots are tender. In small skillet, sauté onion in butter with curry powder, stirring occasionally, until onion is tender (about 5 minutes). In blender or food processor, process ½ of carrot mixture until smooth. Repeat with remaining carrot mixture. Pour into bowl and add onion mixture and yogurt. Mix until smooth. Chill thoroughly. To serve, pour into serving bowls and garnish with cucumber slices and grated carrot.

YIELD: 8 SERVINGS

Easy Strawberry Soup

1 quart fresh strawberries

2 (8 ounce) containers strawberry yogurt

2 tablespoons lemon juice

Wash and hull berries. Set aside a few berries for garnish. In blender or food processor, combine strawberries, yogurt, and lemon juice. Blend until smooth. Chill thoroughly. Serve in chilled serving bowls with sliced berries on top.

YIELD: 8 SERVINGS

Meatball Soup

1 egg

2 cups light cream, divided

1 cup soft bread crumbs

1 small onion, finely chopped

1¾ teaspoons salt, divided

1½ pounds ground beef

1 tablespoon butter

3 tablespoons flour

¾ teaspoon beef bouillon granules

½ teaspoon pepper

¼ teaspoon garlic salt

3 cups water

1 pound red potatoes, cubed

1 (10 ounce) package frozen peas, thawed

In large bowl, beat egg and ⅓ cup cream. Add bread crumbs, onion, and 1 teaspoon salt. Crumble beef over mixture and mix well. Shape into ½-inch balls. In dutch oven, brown meatballs in butter, ½ at a time. Remove from pan. Set aside. Drain fat. To pan, add flour, bouillon, pepper, garlic salt, and remaining ¾ teaspoon salt. Stir until smooth. Gradually stir in water. Bring to boil, stirring often. Add potatoes and meatballs. Reduce heat. Cover and simmer for 25 minutes or until potatoes are tender. Stir in peas and remaining 1⅔ cups cream. Heat thoroughly.

YIELD: 9 SERVINGS

Festive Fresh Fruit Soup

3 tablespoons sugar

3 tablespoons cornstarch

⅛ teaspoon salt

1¼ cups red cooking wine

1 cup water

1½ cups cranberry juice cocktail

1 cup strawberry halves

1 cup seedless green grapes

1 cup cantaloupe, cut into ¼-inch pieces

½ cup sour cream

In 3-quart saucepan, mix sugar, cornstarch, and salt. Stir in wine and water. Heat to boiling, stirring constantly. Boil and stir for 1 minute. Remove from heat. Stir in cranberry juice. Cover loosely and chill thoroughly. Before serving, stir in fruit and garnish with spoon of sour cream.

YIELD: 6 SERVINGS

Dreamy Mushroom Soup

8 ounces fresh mushrooms, divided

4 tablespoons butter, divided

1 medium onion, chopped

¼ cup flour

1 teaspoon salt

¼ teaspoon white pepper

1¼ cups water

1¼ cups chicken broth

1 cup light cream

Slice mushrooms to make 1 cup. Chop up remaining mushrooms. In 3-quart saucepan, sauté sliced mushrooms in 2 tablespoons butter. Remove from pan. In remaining 2 tablespoons butter, sauté chopped mushrooms and onion. Stir in flour, salt, and pepper. Cook over low heat, stirring constantly, until mixture is smooth and bubbly. Remove from heat. Stir in water and broth. Heat to boiling, stirring constantly. Boil and stir for 1 minute. Stir in cream and sliced mushrooms. Heat just until hot.

YIELD: 4 SERVINGS

Hearty Turkey Soup

1 medium onion, chopped

½ cup chopped green bell pepper

3 cloves garlic, minced

1 tablespoon butter

6 cups chicken broth

3 medium carrots, chopped

½ cup dried lentils

1½ teaspoons Italian seasoning

1 teaspoon salt

¼ teaspoon pepper

1 cup cubed turkey

½ cup quick-cooking barley

2 medium mushrooms, chopped

1 (28 ounce) can crushed tomatoes, undrained

In dutch oven, sauté onion, bell pepper, and garlic in butter until tender. Add broth, carrots, lentils, Italian seasoning, salt, and pepper. Bring to boil. Reduce heat. Cover and simmer for 25 minutes. Add turkey, barley, and mushrooms. Return to boil. Reduce heat. Cover and simmer for 15 minutes or until tender. Add tomatoes. Heat thoroughly.

YIELD: 10 SERVINGS

Wintry Wild Rice Soup

2 medium stalks celery, sliced

1 medium carrot, coarsely shredded

½ cup chopped onion

2 small green bell peppers, chopped

2 tablespoons butter

3 tablespoons flour

1 teaspoon salt

¼ teaspoon pepper

1½ cups cooked wild rice

1 cup water

1¼ cups chicken broth

1 cup light cream

⅓ cup slivered almonds, toasted

In 3-quart saucepan, cook and stir celery, carrot, onion, and bell peppers in butter for 5 minutes or until celery is tender. Stir in flour, salt, and pepper. Stir in rice, water, and broth. Heat to boiling and reduce heat. Cover and simmer, stirring occasionally, for 15 minutes. Stir in cream and almonds. Heat to hot (do not boil).

Yield: 5 servings

Creamy Vegetable Soup

2 cups water

1 cup frozen green beans, cut up

¾ cup frozen peas

¼ small head cauliflower, separated
  into florets

2 small carrots, sliced

1 medium potato, cubed

2 cups spinach, cut up

2 cups milk, divided

2 tablespoons flour

¼ cup heavy cream

1½ teaspoons salt

⅛ teaspoon pepper

In 3-quart saucepan, heat water, beans, peas, cauliflower, carrots, and potato. Bring to boil. Reduce heat, cover, and simmer for 10 to 15 minutes or until vegetables are slightly tender. Add spinach. Cook, uncovered, for 1 minute. Mix together ¼ cup milk and flour. Gradually stir into vegetable mixture. Stir in remaining 1¾ cups milk, cream, salt, and pepper. Heat just until hot (do not boil).

YIELD: 6 SERVINGS

Cheddar Cheese Soup

¼ cup chopped onion

½ cup thinly sliced celery

2 tablespoons butter

2 tablespoons flour

¼ teaspoon pepper

¼ teaspoon dry mustard

1 cup milk

1¼ cups chicken broth

2 cups shredded cheddar cheese

In 2-quart saucepan, cook onion and celery in butter for 5 minutes or until tender. Stir in flour, pepper, and mustard. Add milk and broth. Heat to boiling over medium heat, stirring constantly. Boil and stir for 1 minute. Stir in cheese. Heat over low heat, stirring occasionally, until cheese is melted.

Yield: 4 servings

My Favorite Christmas Soup Recipes

Recipe:

INGREDIENTS:

DIRECTIONS:

YIELD:

Recipe:

INGREDIENTS:

DIRECTIONS:

YIELD:

Recipe:

INGREDIENTS:

DIRECTIONS:

YIELD:

Recipe:

INGREDIENTS:

DIRECTIONS:

YIELD:

Recipe:

INGREDIENTS:

DIRECTIONS:

YIELD:

Index

APPETIZERS

BEVERAGES

BREADS

BREAKFAST DISHES

CANDY

COOKIES

DESSERTS

KIDS' RECIPES

MAIN DISHES

SALADS

SIDES

SOUPS